Debbie Weiss

The
Sprinkle
Effect

A Guide to Creating
a More Colorful and Fulfilling Life

Copyright 2024 Maybe I Can, LLC
All rights reserved.

No part of this book may be reproduced in any form or by any electronic or mechanical means, including information storage and retrieval systems, without written permission from the author, except for the use of brief quotations in a book review.

Paperback: 978-1-964924-04-5
Hardcover: 978-1-964924-05-2
Ebook: 978-1-964924-06-9

maybe i can! LLC

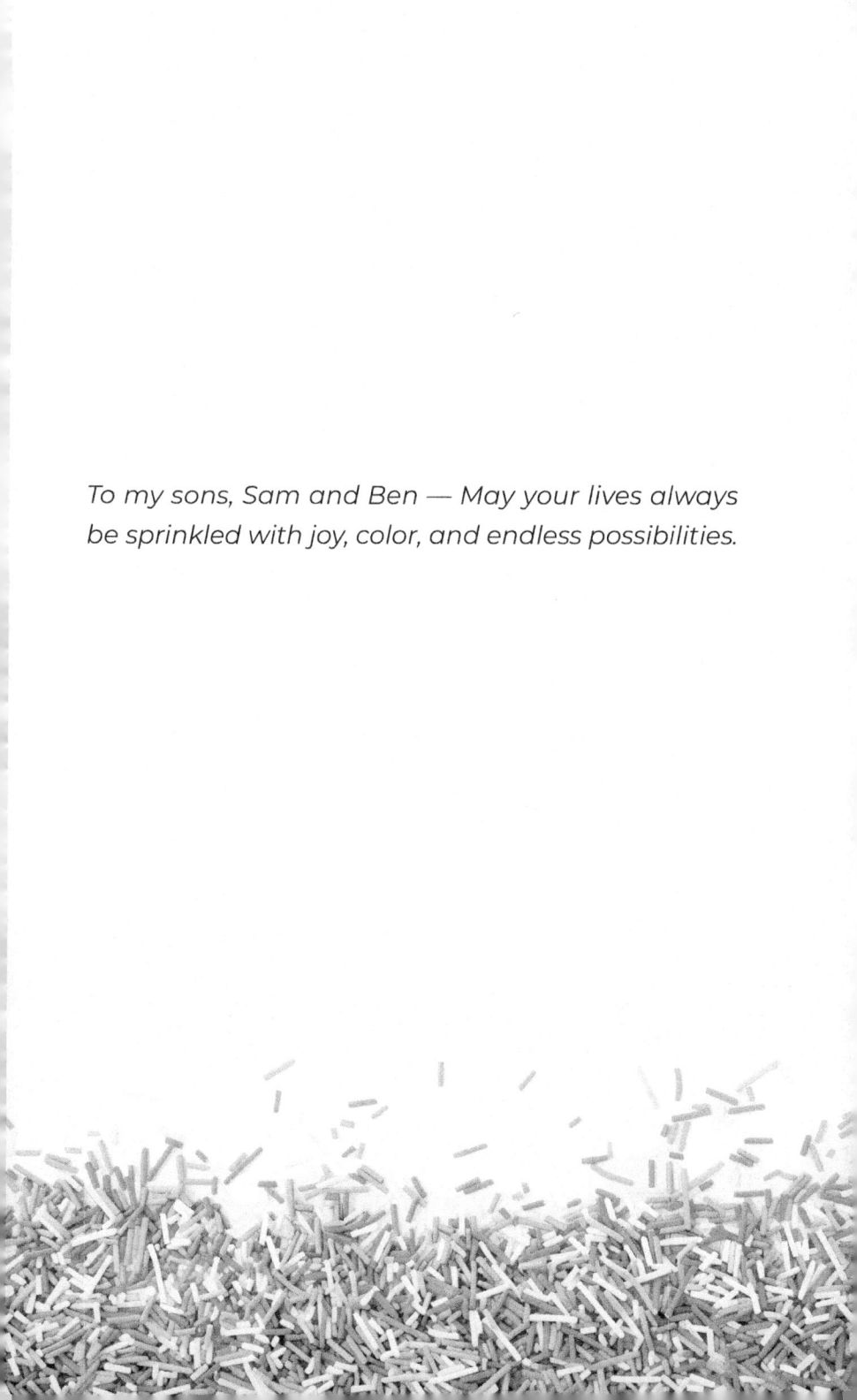

To my sons, Sam and Ben — May your lives always be sprinkled with joy, color, and endless possibilities.

Contents

Preface	7
Introduction: A Sprinkle of Possibilities	9
1. A Sprinkle of Perspective	19
2. A Sprinkle of Mindset	31
3. A Sprinkle of Belief	45
4. A Sprinkle of Courage	57
5. A Sprinkle of Responsibility	67
6. A Sprinkle of Dreams	81
7. A Sprinkle of Direction	91
8. A Sprinkle of Vision	107
9. A Sprinkle of Action	123
10. A Sprinkle of Discipline	133
11. A Sprinkle of Adaptability	147
12. A Sprinkle of Resilience	159
13. A Sprinkle of Curiosity	173
14. A Sprinkle of Connection	187
15. A Sprinkle of Joy	199
Conclusion: A Sprinkle of New Beginnings	213
Acknowledgments	223
About the Author	227

Enhance Your Journey with *The Sprinkle Effect Workbook*!

Deepen your experience with the workbook companion to *The Sprinkle Effect: A Guide to Creating a More Colorful and Fulfilling Life.*

What's Inside:
- Chapter Summaries: Quick recaps of each sprinkle.
- Interactive Activities: All the end-of-chapter activities in one place, with space for your personal answers.
- Exclusive Journal Prompts: Additional prompts to inspire deeper reflection.

Why You'll Love It:
- Practical Application: Move from reading to doing with hands-on activities.
- Personal Growth: Unlock insights and creativity with exclusive prompts.
- Organized Learning: Keep all your reflections and activities together.

Don't just read about a colorful life – start living it!

Scan the QR code or visit debbierweiss.com/books to purchase your workbook today and start your journey towards a more vibrant and fulfilling life!

Preface

    I love rainbow sprinkles. There's something about seeing all those colors adorning my ice cream, cake, or cupcake that makes me happy. Maybe it's all the bright colors or the crunchy, sweet taste. It could be a fond childhood memory that was lost somewhere in this overloaded brain of mine. Of course, the fact that ice cream is my favorite food may also have something to do with it. I'd much rather have sprinkles on top of my ice cream than hot fudge. I know, I know! You might think that's crazy, but you do you.

    It really doesn't matter why or where it came from; I just know sprinkles make me smile. Sprinkles add color, crunch, and decoration to an ordinary dessert, turning it into something extraordinary. Sprinkles have the ability to change my mood, brighten my day, and leave me feeling satisfied. I don't know about you, but I'd like to feel that way all the time.

    There are so many different variations of sprinkles today compared to when I was a kid. We had either chocolate or rainbow sprinkles (or jimmies, depending on where you live). There were no fancy ones in different shapes, textures, or metallic colors. Personally, I still prefer the rainbow sprinkles I grew up with, but it's nice to know that anyone can find a sprinkle that suits their taste.

    This got me thinking: how can I incorporate more sprinkles into my life without adding the calories that come with eating delectable treats day and night? One day, while journaling, the answer appeared in my handwriting, on the page in front of me. I hadn't recalled consciously thinking about this, so I was flabbergasted. Over the last decade, one by one, I have added sprinkles to my life. It had changed my average, okay, run-of-the-mill life into something special.

The sprinkles were no longer in the form of jimmies; instead, they were in the form of gradual changes I've made through mindset shifts, releasing limiting beliefs, and taking action. As I added each new "color" sprinkle, the smile on my face would linger a bit longer each day. I was waking up excited to add a new sprinkle to my ever-increasing jar. My life was growing much more colorful, thanks to *the sprinkle effect*.

How could I keep this secret to myself? I couldn't. I want everyone to add color and crunch to their lives every day, right along with me. You might already possess some of the colors in your metaphorical jar. If so, that's wonderful. Maybe this book will allow you to see that color in a different light. If you need to add a certain color to your sprinkle collection, then I have you covered.

So grab your spoon, ice cream, and jar. Get ready to sprinkle new possibilities into your life, one color at a time.

Introduction

A Sprinkle of Possibilities

LAVENDER:
Associated with creativity and imagination, lavender encompasses the idea of infinite possibilities.

Do you feel like life is passing you by, leaving you caught on a hamster wheel without real progress? Are you unhappy with how things have turned out, perhaps facing a major life transition? Ten years ago, I would have answered "yes" to these questions. I was exhausted, overwhelmed, and resigned to a life that felt out of my control.

Until… I experienced a pivotal moment when I turned fifty (although I didn't realize it at the time). There wasn't any cool music playing in the background, and I didn't suddenly get the guy or a new career. It began with a single thought.

Will I live the rest of my life as I have to this point? Is this all there is?

On paper, my life looked pretty good. I lived in a beautiful house in an idyllic neighborhood with my husband, two sons, and Yogi, our maltipoo. I had my own insurance agency, where both Gary, my husband, and I had worked for the past eighteen years. We had a small team of wonderful people, and it allowed us to live a nice life. *I don't have anything to complain about. There are many other people who would love to trade places with me.*

I was ashamed for even having these thoughts, but just like any picture or social media post, there's so much more behind the story than meets the eye. I was exhausted and lived in a state of constant stress and worry. I didn't know it had a name then, but Gary's struggles with depression and anxiety were intensifying. He was unable to handle so many of the challenges we all face in everyday life, so I was always trying to make things easier for him.

As women often are, I was the master scheduler. My kids were at that age where their activities dictated our lives. We always had somewhere to be: practice, games, school, parties, haircuts, or doctor appointments. In addition to his struggles with mental illness, Gary also had physical illnesses that required attention and a variety of different types of doctors to visit.

Every day I made sure everyone had what they needed. I gave out orders like a drill sergeant, making sure each person was clear on what was happening. However, it was not uncommon to hear "What did you say?" from one or more of the three of them, who all were challenged with ADHD. It was quite frustrating for me. *I'm the one doing it all. All they have to do is listen. Is that asking too much?*

When I wasn't managing the daily household schedule, I was running my office and handling our finances. Of course, our home life did often spill over into our work life since Gary and I worked together and didn't always agree on everything. His depression, anxiety, and ADHD were beginning to affect our employees and customers. I couldn't have that happen, so I tried to do my best to keep everyone happy.

One of the ways I "protected" Gary was by not sharing the financial mess I had gotten us into over the years. He knew some of it, but as it grew more dire, I kept it to myself. Any time I felt the need to share, it would trigger his illness, and he would barely be able to function for days or sometimes weeks. I decided it wasn't worth it. Instead, I would hold it inside and figure out a way to make it all work.

I was an open book with my friends and family when it came to my struggles, except for the money part. I was ashamed and embarrassed of how I had let myself get into such a mess, particularly because I was a CPA and an insurance agent. I should have known better, and I was constantly beating myself up, determined not to let anyone know just how serious it was.

Have you ever kept a secret? One you hoped no one would ever find out? The stress of it is unbearable, so I would do my best to push it out of my mind anytime I started to think about it. I visualized the money secret in a big internal bubble and saw my hand pushing it down into my gut, away from my brain. I had to make it stop; otherwise, I knew I wouldn't survive.

The same year I turned fifty, my eldest son, Sam, turned thirteen. Sam was diagnosed on the autism spectrum at the age of two, adding ADHD (among other diagnoses) at age five and depression at age ten. He was in the throes of puberty and had a tougher time navigating the changes than most other boys his age. I was always worried about him—plotting and planning how I could help him make friends, fit in, and with his academics.

He was (and still is) the sweetest, most loving person I know, but puberty buried those qualities somewhere deep inside. He always seemed to be angry, brooding, and quick to explode. His mouth turned foul, and it felt like we were constantly battling or I was persuading Gary to take it easy on him. Of course, I was also worried about how the "new" Sam was affecting his younger brother, Ben.

On top of all that was going on in my life at that moment, my dad passed away a year and a half earlier. I had become my dad's primary caregiver after he had a massive stroke when I was seventeen, and he had just turned forty-six. He lived for thirty years and was my responsibility.

In my twenties, I had to learn about Medicare, Medicaid, Social Security, and private disability. I learned about doctors and different types of therapies, learning to advocate in hospitals when my dad wasn't getting the attention he needed. I was doing all of this while my friends were living the carefree life you're supposed to be living in your twenties.

As time went on, I began to become a bit resentful of the situation. My dad felt like carrying more weight, and I hated that I felt that way. The guilt turned to silent shame. Logically, I knew none of it was his fault, but seeing others enjoying their lives while I was constantly worried about what my dad needed made me angry. I started to feel sorry for myself, and I found myself at fifty still feeling the same way.

I had spent my adult life taking care of and worrying about everyone and everything else besides myself. Now don't get me wrong; I didn't regret taking care of my dad, husband, and boys, but was caregiving the only thing my life was about? I watched as others seemed to have it all, even though I knew that wasn't exactly true.

Let me just stop right there and tell you that if you had met me then, you would have had no idea what was churning on the inside because I was always a cheery, happy, and positive person. It's not that I wouldn't complain (I did a lot of that to my close friends and family). There always seemed to be some type of chaos, tough situation, or obstacle I needed to maneuver through, and my friends would agree with me that my life was tough and I deserved an award for being so strong and brave.

I had no outlet, no time to truly relax. And then I would compare my life to the lives of those around me. Of course, they had their challenges, but they were mostly brief blips in an otherwise calm life. My challenges had been lifelong with no end in sight. *Why me? What had I done to deserve this kind of life?"*

Some days were easier than others, but there was no real relief. I found myself middle-aged and living a life for everyone else except for *me*. As I mentioned, taking care of my father, my kids, and later my husband is something I would do all over again, but would I do it differently? Absolutely!

Fifty.

Something about that number really got to me. It made me reflect on my mortality and realize that, chances are, I had fewer years ahead of me than I did behind me. I saw how quickly those first fifty years had flown by. I could see how, in a flash, I would be at the end of my life, and I didn't want to be that person who looked back with regrets, saying, *What happened? It all went by so quickly, and I never did what I wanted to do.* Let me tell you, I didn't know what I wanted to do. I had no idea.

It wasn't like I had some pent-up desire to be an artist, doctor, or anything else. I didn't know what I wanted, but I knew there had to be more. I also realized my life was not changing because of some fairy godmother coming down and waving a magic wand. I needed to make those changes myself. Otherwise, fast forward, there I'd be at the end of my days saying, "I wish I would have."

This revelation was overwhelming, eye-opening, and terrifying all at once. *Now, what was I supposed to do about it? How or where do I even start?* I had absolutely no idea. I wished there was some place or someone who could be my guide, but if there was someone, I didn't know where to find them. *What would I even Google?*

For the past ten years, I've been figuring it out on my own—taking some detours, experiencing disappointment, and wondering if I'm on the right path—but it has been exhilarating. For the first time in my life, I've discovered what it is to actually live, and it's the best feeling ever! Instead of keeping my head down and plowing through my daily tasks, I've become intentional about what I want my days to look like. I've pushed through my fear and taken chances I never would have in the past.

This has allowed me to discover new passions and abilities that had been hiding deep inside. My confidence and courage have soared, and I've realized I have the freedom to live my life as I want, regardless of everyone and everything else going on around me. A new world of infinite possibilities suddenly appeared. My journey isn't over; it will continue until I take my last breath, but I want to share with you what I've learned thus far and be your guide—the guide I never had—to help you begin to live the life that you want, even if you don't know what you want it to look like.

Personal development or personal growth were bookstore aisles I would ignore in the past. It seemed like a bunch of nonsense, or for people who needed help or were "out there," if you know what I mean. *Who had time to waste with that nonsense?* I had real problems that needed addressing, and I had no time to waste on soul-searching. Looking back, I'm embarrassed to admit these feelings.

Once I jumped in, it felt like I had entered an alternate reality. I had become Dorothy in *The Wizard of Oz*, and everyone was living life differently. They thought and talked about things I had never heard of or didn't really know anything about. There was so much to take in that I didn't know where to start. There were too many options and mountains of information to digest. No one answer is right, and everyone starts from a different place, but after being on this adventure for a decade, I want to provide a roadmap for you to use as you see fit.

I'm not a psychologist, scientist, or researcher, so you will not hear much about case studies to validate the points made. Instead, I will share the most helpful and valuable lessons I have learned during my decade of self-discovery in a relatable, easy-to-understand way. This is a beginner's guide to creating the life you want. It's an introduction to concepts and ideas that, when put into practice, will change your life forever.

Warning: This requires work on your part. You cannot just read this book and not be an active participant. Only **you** can decide how you want the rest of your story to unfold, not me. I will provide the framework and exercises, but **you** are the one who has to commit to the process.

How many times have you wished you had a magic wand or your own genie that could give you what you wanted? I have certainly done my fair share of wishing, so you're not alone. I've come to realize that even if Amazon delivered a genie in a bottle to my doorstep, it wouldn't be the same as doing it myself. It is the process of learning and discovering ourselves, our dreams, and our desires; that is just as, or even more, satisfying than having what we want.

What you want could be physical items like a certain car, vacation home, or diamond ring. There's nothing wrong with that, and I'm not going to lie, there are possessions that I want, too. However, it's more than just *things*. It could be the quality of your relationships or the ratio of time you spend working versus being with loved ones. Maybe it's your health and wellness or the impact you want to have on others. The possibilities are unlimited. It's all up to you. So find a quiet place where you can read and complete the activities and journal prompts.

If the idea of a journal prompt is new to you, don't be intimidated. It's basically a question you ask yourself, and instead of saying it out loud or thinking about it, you write your answer down on a blank piece of paper. You might be tempted, as I used to be, to just think about your answer, but the act of putting pen to paper is much more impactful. Completing these exercises will take you on your own journey of self-discovery. They are the most crucial part of this book because they allow you to put the concepts learned into practice.

If you don't have time to complete the exercises in their entirety as you go through the book, schedule a time to do so. Believe me, I've been there and done that. I've been on both ends of the spectrum. I've read books and haven't done the work, and while I appreciated the message, once I was done reading, I forgot everything I learned. It was only when I was an active participant and really put the time in that I started to see results. It will make it easier to have all your answers in one place, so I recommend using a new notebook or *The Sprinkle Effect Workbook*, which you can purchase by scanning the QR code in the front of the book.

Just as there are a variety of sprinkles, there are a variety of ways you can use this book:

1. Read it from cover to cover without stopping to do the exercises. You can then go back and slowly tackle the exercises you feel you need.

2. Read a chapter and do the exercises at the end before moving on to the next chapter. I recommend taking some time before moving forward so you have enough time to digest that particular sprinkle.

3. Only read the chapters you feel you need. Maybe you already have orange, teal, and blue in your jar, so skip to the colors you desire the most.

4. Once you're done and have the whole rainbow in your jar, refer back to your prompts and answers when it feels like one of the colors is dimming.

Okay, I've done enough preaching…wait, one more thing. I want you to remember why you picked up this book. I'm guessing there's a little voice inside of you whispering in your ear, wondering if it's possible for you to design a life you truly love. This book will give you the tools necessary to do just that. You are motivated to make a change, so now let's make it happen!

1

A Sprinkle of Perspective

BLUE:
Often associated with depth and stability, blue can represent a broad and deep perspective.

Have you ever had that experience where you've looked at a situation or thought one way, assuming that's the correct view, until something hits you and you come to the realization there might be a different way to look at it? You then wonder how you didn't see it that way before. It now seems so obvious! Regardless of how many times this happens, we still have a tendency to have tunnel vision and think there is only one correct answer, and our answer is obviously right. That is, until the next time it smacks us in the face.

In June 2022, Gary, my husband, received a terminal cancer diagnosis, which obviously turned my world upside down in every way. My typical routines quickly disappeared as I was forced to take on new caregiving responsibilities. I had run my insurance agency since 1995 and was the kind of employer who was in the trenches with my employees. I came to work at the same time and often left later than they did. I took a similar amount of vacation time as well.

I was there, listening to them talk to customers and giving them feedback about the interaction. I was monitoring our activity and sales numbers on a regular basis, having impromptu meetings to discuss and strategize. I was there to help with any question, and I was always quick to jump in to help or provide the answer, even if someone didn't ask me directly.

In my mind, I thought if I wasn't there as much or more than my team, they would think I didn't care or was taking advantage of them. I hated the idea that they might think I was just doing this to make money and not take my responsibility for them and my customers seriously. If I had to take off or leave for some reason, I always felt the need to explain to them why I wouldn't be there. It was almost like I was asking their permission so they wouldn't judge me.

For the last half of 2022, I was forced to change. Caring for Gary required my constant attention. He wasn't able to function because of both physical and mental illnesses. I took him to doctor appointments, gave him pills five times a day, and was there day and night for anything he needed. I rarely went to the office. Most weeks, I was able to pop in for a few hours. I would check in with them most days, and I was always a phone call away if they needed me, but I did not work. At first, I was beside myself, stressing out over how I could possibly do it all. My team of four wonderful, amazing, caring women assured me that they had the office covered and that I shouldn't give it a second thought. It took me a month or two to let go of the guilt.

My family was who I needed to focus on, and as the months became more challenging as Gary deteriorated, it was easier for me to let go and not think about my agency. I developed new daily habits and routines. One of them was finding an hour for myself each day. A year or so prior, I began to explore other business ideas, including writing my memoir, and with time away from my agency, it was nice to be able to focus more on becoming an author since I didn't need to physically be at an office to do so.

Six months later, my caregiving ended when Gary lost his battle with cancer on December 30, 2022. I no longer had an excuse to stay home, although I found myself wanting to remain there. I liked being able to work on my new business without the distractions of my agency, but I no longer had an excuse. *What would they think of me? They had already gone above and beyond the call of duty, and now I wanted more? How selfish of me!* The passion I had for my new project would have to be put on hold, or at least minimized, until the time was right.

So I went back to work. The first day, I sat down with Mary Jo, who had worked for me for over twenty years. She had been in charge in my absence. I wanted to thank her and find out how challenging the last six months had been for her. When I asked, I was absolutely shocked by her one-word answer: empowering. I certainly did not see that one coming. I assumed she would tell me the difficulties she encountered, but I knew she wouldn't complain. She was so kind, and she would do anything for Gary or me. But, in my wildest dreams, I would never have thought she actually liked not having me there. I know that's not exactly what she said, but it was in a way.

In all these years, she was never given a chance to lead because I had always been there to answer every question and fix every problem. I did the same for her, too. It's always easier to go ask someone for the answer instead of having to figure it out yourself, and that's the culture I created. It hadn't dawned on me that Mary Jo and the rest of my team thought I didn't trust them because of my micromanaging and always jumping in with a solution.

Now, I can certainly understand their perspective, and because I do, I've changed how I operate. I no longer keep the same hours they do and am not so quick to give them the answers. Thanks to my change of perspective, we all have more freedom and power over our actions.

Our perspective comes from the sum of our beliefs, values, and experiences. All those things become the lens, the glasses, that we look through as we live life.

Where did my original perspective that, in order to be a good boss, I needed to be a micromanager come from anyway? Our perspective comes from the sum of our beliefs, values, and experiences. All those things become the lens, the glasses, that we look through as we live life. The funny thing is, we don't realize each of us are wearing different glasses, and we can take them off and try on a different pair. If you think about it, each of us experiences every little thing differently because we're each seeing it through our own lens or perspective.

Why do we assume we are the ones wearing the correct glasses? Maybe our friend is. Or our enemy. Or none of us are right. It's just different.

I don't know about you, but I can think of countless situations where I've tried to convince someone I was

> **Why do we assume we are the ones wearing the correct glasses? Maybe our friend is. Or our enemy. Or none of us are right. It's just different.**

right, as if my life depended on it. It would infuriate me if I couldn't make someone come around to my point of view. I was so darn sure I was right and had no idea why the other person could think any differently. That person was most likely thinking the same about me.

Just imagine if inventors or explorers accepted the status quo or current perspective. Albert Einstein changed the world of physics with his theory of relativity. He introduced a new way to think about time and space. Steve Jobs changed the perspective that phones are just for talking. Thanks to him, we can conduct personal and professional business anytime through the small handheld device we carry around.

If I hadn't had another shift in perspective a decade ago, you wouldn't be reading this book right now. My opinion about most everything you'll read in this book was that it was a bunch of nonsense. The personal development industry was geared towards those who were looking for someone to tell them what to do, sort of like a cult. I'm not sure where that belief came from, but it was most likely based on what others around me said. It might have stemmed from the fact that I was a child in the sixties and the people in my world didn't have a positive view of hippies. I'm so grateful that I have had a massive perspective shift and realized that personal growth is not just for hippies; it's for all of us. It should be a required course taught in schools everywhere, and my goal is to bring this information to the masses.

The beginning of transforming your life begins with a willingness to see that there just might be another way. I've realized that seeing things from a different perspective isn't just about changing your view, it's about opening doors to growth and new possibilities. Whether it's rethinking how we work or seeing the strengths in those around us, each shift can lead to richer, more fulfilling experiences. Our perspectives shape our world and changing them can transform our lives in incredible ways.

Are you ready to begin your journey?

I've realized that seeing things from a different perspective isn't just about changing your view, it's about opening doors to growth and new possibilities.

Key Takeaways:

1. **Perspective Shapes Our Reality:** Changing how we view our roles and responsibilities can profoundly impact our happiness and effectiveness.

2. **Embracing Different Viewpoints:** Recognizing that others may have valid perspectives can broaden our understanding and enrich our interactions.

3. **Openness to New Perspectives Is Key:** Being willing to reconsider our viewpoints can lead to significant personal growth and improved relationships.

Activities

Activity 1: Reframing Exercise: Shifting Perspective

Objective
Practice the skill of reframing by changing negative or unhelpful thoughts into more positive, empowering ones.

Step 1: Identify the Negative Thought

Write down a specific negative thought you've had recently. It could be about yourself, your abilities, a situation at work, or a personal relationship.

Example: *"I never do anything right."*

Step 2: Challenge the Thought

Ask yourself a series of questions to challenge this thought. Is it really true? What evidence do I have to support this thought? Is there evidence that contradicts this thought?

Example Questions:

Have there really been no instances where I've done something right?

Can I think of a time when I succeeded at something or received positive feedback?

Step 3: Identify the Trigger

Reflect on what triggered this negative thought. Understanding the context can help you see patterns and situations that often lead to negative thinking.

Example Trigger: Maybe the thought arises when you're trying a new task at work or after a conversation with a particular person.

Step 4: Reframe the Thought

Transform the negative thought into a more positive or neutral one. The reframed thought should be believable and based in reality. It's not about creating a false sense of positivity but rather finding a more balanced view.

Reframed Thought Example: "While I sometimes make mistakes, I also have successes. Everyone has areas to improve, and I'm working on mine. I learn from my mistakes and celebrate my achievements."

Step 5: Reflect on the Reframe

Consider how the reframed thought makes you feel compared to the original negative thought. Does it reduce stress? Does it feel more empowering? Reflection can help reinforce the value of reframing.

Activity 2: Media Diversity Audit

Objective

Broaden your understanding and perspective by exposing yourself to different viewpoints and cultural narratives through diverse media sources.

For one week, consume media only from sources outside your usual choices (e.g., if you usually watch mainstream news, try independent outlets; if you read Western authors, choose authors from other parts of the world). Note any differences in viewpoints and information presented.

Activity 3: Empathy Exercise

Objective
Practice seeing situations from another person's perspective to enhance empathy and understanding.

Step 1: Identify a Situation

Think of a recent conflict or misunderstanding you had with someone. It could be a minor disagreement or a more significant issue.

Step 2: Write Your Perspective

Write down your perspective of the situation. Describe what happened, how you felt, and why you felt that way.

Step 3: Shift to Their Shoes

Now, write down the same situation from the other person's perspective. Imagine their feelings, thoughts, and motivations. Why might they have acted or reacted the way they did?

Step 4: Find Common Ground

Identify any common ground or shared feelings between your perspective and theirs. What can you learn from seeing things from their point of view?

Step 5: Reflect on the Experience

Write a reflection on what you learned from this exercise. Did it change your understanding of the situation? How can this new perspective help in future interactions?

Journal Prompt

Identify a major life change you've experienced. Write a few sentences on how your perspective shifted before and after this change. What new insights did you gain?

2

A Sprinkle of Mindset

SILVER:
Shiny and reflective, silver sprinkles can symbolize the clarity and brightness of a positive mindset.

I was ready to test out this new perspective thing but had no idea where to start. It turns out that listening to a podcast helped me figure this out. So, true confession time—I really didn't understand how podcasts worked. My college roommate, Mary, would always mention what she was listening to, and I was too embarrassed to ask her the questions that were going through my head:

Who were these mysterious "podcast people" she was listening to? What value could she get from strangers who aren't even famous or considered experts? How did you even find the podcasts you were listening to?

One day, I mustered up the courage and questioned her. She explained how to do a search and gave me a little background on who, about what, and why she listened. She and I don't have similar tastes, so she wasn't much help in steering me towards a show. The only thing I could think to search for was "weight loss," since that was the burning topic forever on my mind. I started and quickly stopped listening to a few shows that either didn't interest me or I didn't connect with the host. I settled on one show where I couldn't decide whether I liked it or not but was willing to put in the time to listen.

In one of the episodes, the host introduced her guest as if she were the Queen of England. Her name was Elizabeth Benton, and I had never heard of her, but based on the introduction, I believed I should have. Elizabeth had lost over 150 pounds and had paid off $130,000 of debt, all by shifting her mindset.

Well, not only did I still want to lose weight, but I was also drowning in debt. Elizabeth was speaking my language. She had experience, and I wanted to learn from her. It turned out she also had a podcast called "Primal Potential," and I quickly became an avid listener. I listened to her whenever I was driving which, was a big change for me since music had kept me company in the car since the day I got behind the wheel.

Elizabeth shared different tips and tricks, and I really resonated with most of the things she said. She started to talk about this course she was offering that would help you begin to transform your life. *Well, sign me up!* At least that's what I was thinking until I saw the price tag. It was $1,200 for a twelve-week course. I couldn't believe how expensive it was. I had never thought in my wildest dreams that it would cost that much money. I started to think it was a scam and began to try and catch Elizabeth in some type of lie that would reveal that both she and her course were fake—a fraud.

I still listened to her, and each episode, I would consider the course yet again. I decided that the one thing I would focus on if I were to take the course was my money issues.

It seemed quite illogical to put myself in further debt to try and figure out how to get out of debt. However, something kept bringing me back to her website and the enrollment page. I realized that my life was not unfolding how I wanted it to, and by following the same patterns I had in the past, nothing would change.

I had already proven to myself how powerful my thoughts were by changing my perspective about self-care, but I wasn't sure how changing my mindset about money was going to change my suffocating financial situation. All I knew was that I hadn't been able to figure it out on my own, and if I didn't do something differently, I was headed for deep trouble. *Elizabeth did it, so why can't I?*

I took a leap of faith and enrolled in her twelve-week course, although I was still skeptical. I was convinced I had thrown away money on an empty sales pitch. I was waiting for proof that I had made a mistake once again with my money, confirming there was no way out. The course felt like it started off a bit slowly, and I wasn't seeing any value. It consisted of a weekly training video, daily journal, and weekly Q&A sessions with Elizabeth.

The daily journal stressed me out. I had never journaled before, and there were prompts I didn't really understand. Even though no one else would see my journal, my need to be an A student would take over, and I approached the process of answering journal questions as if I were being tortured. In the Q&A sessions, it became apparent that I was not the only one suffering just by looking at the journal. I wanted Elizabeth to simply tell me what I should write in there, but she never did. She told us to relax and stop judging ourselves. There was no right or wrong. The journal was personal to each individual.

Elizabeth's answer annoyed me, but I paid the money, so I tried to get on board with the journaling. As the weeks went on, I had a better feel for how I wanted to use the journal and found that it was no longer torture but instead something I looked forward to each morning. Each week, the videos provided different challenges and areas of focus. I joined hoping Elizabeth was going to tell me step by step how to resolve my money mess, but that's not what I got.

Instead, I was given questions to reflect on. I resisted doing this because I thought it was just filler content and a waste of my time. The answer was simple; all I needed to do was change my mindset. Of course, this is *much* easier said than done, and I wasn't sold on the idea. I was so confused over all these different terms that were being thrown around, like mindfulness, mediation, and mindset. *Are they the same thing? Which one do I choose, and how do I begin?*

Tony Robbins, a renowned life coach and motivational speaker, defines mindset as follows: "Your mindset is the driving force behind everything you do. It determines how you perceive situations, how you approach challenges, and ultimately, how you succeed or fail. A positive mindset can transform obstacles into opportunities, while a negative mindset can turn opportunities into obstacles."

"Your mindset is the driving force behind everything you do. It determines how you perceive situations, how you approach challenges, and ultimately, how you succeed or fail."

Tony Robbins

It's your attitude toward just about everything. Mindset is where the magic happens. It's the difference between living the life you desire and the one that sort of happens. It sounds a bit dramatic, but it's true. I never really understood the power or deeper meaning of mindset. The only thing mindset used to mean to me was having a more positive outlook on life. Of course, that is part of it, but you have so much more power than that. Mindset is how you think about everything—things you aren't even aware that you're thinking.

One of the first aha moments I had around this topic was the fact that my thoughts are not necessarily true. *WHAT? If a thought crosses my mind, it must be true.* I don't know where my belief came from, but what I do know is that I never challenged my thoughts. I honestly never thought to question myself because I never realized I was actually lying to myself about so many different things.

The lies were mostly about the limitations I was putting on myself. I had a laundry list of reasons why I could never do or achieve certain things. I told myself that it was impossible. I wasn't good enough, smart enough, knowledgeable enough, or lucky enough. My life was destined to be however it played out, and I just needed to accept it. So I did, until I didn't!

In Carol S. Dweck's book, *Mindset: The New Psychology of Success*, she explains that there are two types of mindsets: fixed and growth. "People with a fixed mindset believe that they're born with certain intelligence, skills and abilities that cannot change." This is exactly what I used to think about my potential and my life. I had no idea that my way of thinking had an actual name.

According to Dweck, "In a growth mindset, people believe that their most basic abilities can be developed through dedication and hard work—brains and talent are just the starting point. This view creates a love of learning and a resilience that is essential for great accomplishment." Dweck believes that most of us are a combination of the two different mindsets. Adopting a growth mindset can improve every aspect of our lives. We can become more resilient, lower stress, and improve relationships. Our careers can benefit, and our sense of fulfillment and life satisfaction can soar. I don't know about you, but all that sounds pretty good to me! The key is to move ourselves from a fixed mindset to a growth mindset.

This is where mindfulness and meditation come into play. The Merriam-Webster dictionary defines mindfulness as:

1. the quality or state of being **mindful**

2. the practice of maintaining a nonjudgmental state of heightened or complete awareness of one's thoughts, emotions, or experiences on a moment-to-moment basis"

It is training ourselves to live in the present moment and become aware of our thoughts. There are various tools that we can use to help us develop a practice of mindfulness, including but not limited to:

- meditating
- focusing on our breathing
- journaling
- practicing gratitude

- being present
- single-tasking instead of multi-tasking

I still didn't believe that doing any of these things made sense. *How is focusing on my breathing going to change my life?* I couldn't take a few deep breaths and have my troubles disappear. If only it were that easy. My life was complicated, and I still couldn't understand how any of these actions could help me change anything.

If I'm being honest, I thought it was all a bit too "woo-woo" for me. I wasn't sold on any of this yet...

So I started with where I was comfortable: books. I started reading and listening to different audiobooks that either spoke about mindset or highlighted someone's inspirational story. The more I read about others overcoming their challenges, the more I began to believe the same was possible for me.

I reflected on those times in my life when I had an "I can't" attitude, which were too many to count. I made a list of all the things I had done when I initially thought, "I can't." I call it my "Maybe I Can" list, and here are some of the things on it:

1. Go on without Bobby, my first love and fiancé, who broke up with me to be with someone else.
2. Go away to college a second time.
3. Advocate on behalf of my dad.
4. Change professions when I had no idea what I was doing and all I wanted to do was quit.

5. Allow Gary to give me injections (a requirement when going through the IVF journey).

6. Give birth.

7. Figure out how to deal with my ten-year-old son, who told me he wanted to die.

These are only a few, but you get the idea. Each time I think I am incapable of doing something, I refer to this list and think about how I initially felt the same way in all these situations, but in the end, I not only survived but often thrived. Just glancing at the "Maybe I Can" list reminds me I am so much stronger than I give myself credit for. As I reflect, I am also struck by the fact that getting through all these challenges has made me the person I am today, and I wouldn't want to change a thing.

> **A big part of a growth mindset is to be uncomfortable and do it anyway.**

Scary things are scary. Profound, right? They are, and in the short term, it's so much easier to retreat and curl up in your bed under the covers, but if we do that, we wouldn't be living and progressing. A big part of a growth mindset is to be uncomfortable and do it anyway. My list proves this concept. All the things on my list had, in turn, given me the greatest gifts of my life.

I remember being petrified before I gave birth to my oldest son. The thought that got me through was that all the other mothers in the world had done it, and they seemed to be doing okay. If they could do it, I could too. Sure, many moms have their own birthing horror stories, but they survived. Keeping the baby inside of me indefinitely was clearly not an option, so I calmed myself down remembering all the others who went through the same thing, even though they were terrified.

I now apply this phrase to anything that scares me. Each time I make another entry on my list, it reinforces the fact that I can do it, and if I can do it, you can too!

Here are a few steps you can take to change from a fixed mindset to a growth mindset:

1. Try new activities that are challenging. This will help you to increase your confidence and change the way you think about yourself.

2. Give yourself credit for trying, even if it doesn't work out. View mistakes as learning opportunities, not failure or a character flaw.

3. Believe in yourself and your ability to grow and change. If there's something you can't do, it doesn't mean it will always be that way; it means you just can't do it YET!

4. Celebrate your progress. If you spent an hour practicing piano, make sure to give yourself a big pat on the back. That's a win!

Even though Elizabeth never gave me step-by-step instructions on how to pay off my debt, what she gave me was something even better: the power to change the way I think, which in turn will change my behavior and actions. I can make this happen with a mindset shift. Carol Dweck's research shows that adults are capable of changing their mindset; they just need to make the effort and focus on it.

Remember that our thoughts really shape our lives. Every challenge is a chance to learn and grow.

> **Every challenge is a chance to learn and grow.**

Changing how you think isn't just about quick fixes—it's about understanding yourself better and making changes that last. This is a lifelong process, and we need to be consciously aware of whether what we're thinking about is consistent with the direction we want to go in life.

Keep using what you've learned about mindset as you move forward. It's a journey that involves checking in with yourself and being open to change. Keep working on seeing things differently and taking on challenges as opportunities to get better. Believe in your ability to change, stay curious, and use your new perspective to guide you toward the life you want. Keep pushing, keep growing, and trust in the power of your own thoughts to change your path.

Key Takeaways:

1. **Transformative Power of Mindset:** Shifting from a fixed to a growth mindset expands possibilities and impacts outcomes.

2. **Challenges as Growth Opportunities:** Embrace challenges as chances to learn and grow, not just obstacles.

3. **Importance of Self-Awareness:** Use tools like journaling and mindfulness to increase self-awareness and guide your mindset transformation.

Activities

Activity 1: Create Your Own "Maybe I Can" List

Objective

Reflect on your past achievements and survivals to build confidence and resilience. Keep this list accessible for moments when you need a reminder of your capabilities and growth.

Make a list of all the things in your life that you survived and/or accomplished. I recommend keeping the list somewhere easily accessible such as on your phone or computer so you can refer back to it often.

Activity 2: The Power of Yet

Objective

Shift your mindset from fixed to growth by adding "yet" to self-limiting statements. Track these instances and reflect weekly to recognize how this small change impacts your perception of challenges.

Whenever you catch yourself saying "I can't do this," add "yet" to the end. Write down these instances and reflect on them at the end of the week. How does adding "yet" change your feelings about the challenges?

Activity 3: Skill Development Commitment

Objective

Break through the fear of failure by committing to a new skill or habit, dedicating manageable time segments consistently over three weeks.

Pick a new skill or habit you've wanted to learn or incorporate into your life but have avoided due to fear of failure. Dedicate a small, manageable amount of time three days a week to learning this skill. Commit to trying this for three weeks. Document your progress and setbacks, focusing on what you learn from each.

Journal Prompt

Describe a time when you encountered a challenge and felt defeated. How might approaching this challenge with a growth mindset change your perspective and actions?

3

A Sprinkle of Belief

GOLD:
Precious and valuable, gold represents the foundational beliefs that support and enrich our lives.

So now that you believe in the power of your thoughts, it's time to start making things happen. Maybe you've had a time in your life where you believed in yourself, but then the excuses started flooding your mind like a tidal wave. You're telling yourself all the reasons why you're not capable, worthy, smart, deserving, or some other excuse. We all do it. All these excuses we tell ourselves are called limiting beliefs. These thoughts can stop you from doing things you are capable of. They are false accusations that you've been telling yourself, and due to the repetition of these thoughts over time, you have grown to believe they are true. These beliefs developed over the course of your life but most likely originated during childhood.

> **All these excuses we tell ourselves are called limiting beliefs. These thoughts can stop you from doing things you are capable of.**

We acquired these beliefs from the people around us, like our parents, teachers, and peers. Now, I'm not saying that they told you flat out that you were not worthy of love or not good enough (although maybe they did). It could have been subtle in the way you interpreted their words and actions. Most likely, it was not on purpose, and they had no idea how what they were saying or doing was impacting you.

According to Gay Hendricks, PhD, in his book *The Big Leap* there are four types of limiting beliefs:

1. Feeling flawed and unworthy of success

2. Fear of disloyalty and abandonment

3. Fear of the burdens of success

4. Fear of surpassing others

Most of us have at least one of these fears or beliefs. When I look at the list, it's obvious to me that I've always felt flawed and unworthy. I was constantly judged for the way I looked. I was a chubby little girl living in a family of thin people, surrounded by other thin little girls. My earliest memories are from preschool, knowing I didn't look like the others. I was different, and I didn't want to be. I wanted to look and be like everyone else.

The teasing began in elementary school. Kids would say things behind my back or right to my face, calling me fatso, thunder thighs, or big mama. When I was in third grade, there was a girl named Nora who was relentless. She took such obvious pleasure in reminding me that I was not good enough. She would torture me when I walked home from school by following me and continuously calling me names.

In the winter, I had a forest green coat. She would steal chalk from school and chase me on the walk home, writing all over my coat with the chalk. I would try to run away, but I was slow, and she wasn't. I would cry, and she would call me a baby, in addition to all the other versions of fatso she could think of. It was unbearable, and I dreaded when the bell rang and it was time to go home. *What have I done to deserve this? Why is this happening to me?*

I would cry to my parents. They tried to teach me to stand up for myself, but she was such a bully, and I was so timid. Eventually, my mother had to intercede and speak to Nora's mother. Once that happened, the torture on the walk home ended, but the name-calling didn't. Nora wasn't the only one. It felt like everyone at school, at one point or another, would join in the teasing. Once someone started, then everyone else would laugh and add their own remarks.

It wasn't just the kids; adults were judging me as well; they just tried to hide it. The looks and the little comments added up. The world sent me a message, and I received it loud and clear: *I didn't measure up. I didn't deserve the life everyone else was living because I was weak. I couldn't control my weight.*

My parents didn't know how to help since neither of them had to deal with a weight issue. So they would put me on these very restrictive diets, and I would be successful for a few weeks, or maybe a few months, until I could no longer stand the deprivation. They would hide the chips and cookies all around the house so I wouldn't see them. Of course, when I did happen to come across some hidden snack, I couldn't control myself and would eat the majority of the bag or box. After all, I never knew when or if I would ever find that treat again. After the binge, I would berate myself, deciding that this was proof I was not worthy. I was weak and had no willpower. At that point, the diet was over. The floodgates would open, I would look for any food I had not been able to eat, and all the weight would pile back on.

My life continued in a similar fashion. I would start to feel better about myself each time I lost some weight. I would hold myself differently, have more confidence, and want to be seen instead of trying to hide so no one would notice me. I loved the praise I received from everyone about how great I looked, and they would always tell me to keep going and that they were so proud of me. My chest would puff up with pride, and I would dream about the day that I would reach my goal and my life would be completely different.

Boy, did those moments feel good, until something derailed me and I fell off the wagon. Once I ate something I wasn't supposed to, it sparked a reminder of just how good these forbidden foods tasted, and since I had already messed up, I might as well keep going and eat what I want. *I'll just eat this one thing and then I'll stop. I'll get back on track tomorrow. I'll start over next week.* Most of the time, I did not get back on track. Those very restrictive diets were excruciating. The food I was allowed to eat was bland and gross, and as a teenager, I would watch my friends eat whatever they wanted as I sat there, tortured because I couldn't or shouldn't.

This became the pattern of my life, even as an adult. As a matter of fact, I still struggle today. Even though I've developed a much healthier relationship with food, my confidence level soars when I'm feeling good about my body. It takes daily practice to shift that mindset. In my mind, I have proof that I'm only worthy if I'm thin, and by thin, I mean like a size ten or twelve, which is hardly considered thin by most in today's world, but to me it is. I can still hear Nora and all the other kids calling me names—chasing, torturing, and reminding me that I wasn't like them and that I wasn't good enough.

But is that true? Does my weight struggle define me? Other people have struggles too; their struggles are just different. So does that mean they aren't good enough either?

Nora probably called me names a hundred times; however, since those days, I've repeated that same thought to myself thousands of times. I wasn't able to stop Nora, but I have the power to stop myself. In the book *Don't Believe Everything You Think*, Joseph Nguyen says, "If your mind is completely full of old thinking, it is impossible to have any new thoughts come into your mind to create the change you seek." In other words, it's up to us. I've blamed Nora for most of my life, but in actuality, it is me who continues this narrative.

You need to identify the stories you're telling yourself. Come on, you know what I mean, because we all have them. You just don't want to think about it because it's painful. Who wants to revisit those times in their life when they were made to feel bad about themselves? However, this is exactly what you need to do, because once you do, you can begin

You need to identify the stories you're telling yourself.

to release them. They are not true, and they are stopping you from living life to the fullest.

These beliefs are simply thoughts you've been thinking about over and over again, so you believe them to be true. One of the great things about our brain is that it is neuroplastic, so we have the ability to reprogram it regardless of our age. You can start by being aware when those old stories pop up in your mind by reminding yourself that they are not true and replacing them with a new story.

Think about the areas in your life where you are successful. What story do you tell yourself about that as compared to the things that present a challenge? For example, I tell myself that I'm smart and capable of running a business, and that is why I'm successful in my career. However, I also tell myself that I have to stress over money just like my parents have. It then makes sense to me why my relationship with money doesn't change.

Instead, I can change my story: I am intelligent and have all the skills necessary to change my relationship with money. Imagine how I would begin to act differently. With the first story, why would I even try to do anything differently? The more we tell ourselves the same story over and over again, the more we believe it and automatically make decisions that support it. Depending on your story, this can either work for us or against us.

These beliefs are simply thoughts you've been thinking about over and over again, so you believe them to be true. One of the great things about our brain is that it is neuroplastic, so we have the ability to reprogram it regardless of our age.

When I was about to publish my memoir, *On Second Thought... Maybe I Can!* I had the opportunity to have Jack Canfield, the co-author of the *Chicken Soup for the Soul®* series, read my book. When I met him virtually, I introduced myself as a numbers girl. I told him how I had always been a numbers girl, not a words girl. I went on and on about how I was a CPA and an insurance agent, and I never had a desire to write anything.

In college, I would actually try to avoid registering for classes that had term papers as a requirement. This was absolutely the story that I believed, and before he could critique my memoir, I wanted to make sure he was aware that I was not a writer, so he should have very low expectations about the quality of my book.

When I was done telling my story, my heart was pounding out of my chest, waiting to hear what Jack had to say. I knew that I had opened the door for him; he could easily agree with me. I wished that I was never given the opportunity to have him read my book. *What was I thinking? Why did I sign up to be humiliated?*

I tried to hide the shock on my face when he told me that I was wrong and that I should never refer to myself as just a numbers girl again. I was a number AND WORDS girl. *Excuse me? What did he just say?* He continued on, telling me all the things he enjoyed about the book and how he found it *delightful*.

Did you hear me scream once I clicked on the "leave meeting" button? According to Jack, I was telling myself the wrong story. *If an author of his stature validates my writing, then why can't I?* This is a limiting belief I still struggle with. I seem to always compare my writing to that of those who are considered to be literary greats, but the funny thing is, I don't like to read those types of books. I like to read something that's easy to digest with a voice I can relate to, so why aren't there other people out there who feel the same way?

It was this story that helped me write my memoir as well as this book. If I had stuck with my original "numbers girl" story, you wouldn't be reading this right now. It's pretty powerful to think that this book wouldn't exist if I hadn't changed my story.

Now it's time to figure out what stories you are telling yourself.

Here are some common examples to give you food for thought:

- I don't have time.
- I'm too old to learn or try anything new.
- I'm not strong enough.
- I'm not capable.
- I'm not worthy of being loved.

Are any of those a trigger for you? It's time to take out that pen and paper and answer some questions that will help you recognize beliefs that stop you from achieving what you want.

Key Takeaways:

1. Spotting Limiting Beliefs: The reasons we often doubt ourselves, like feeling scared or not good enough, develop early and stem from what we learn from parents, teachers, and friends.

2. Changing Our Brain: Our brain can learn new ways of thinking, which means we can change old doubts into positive thoughts that help us do better.

3. Being Honest with Ourselves: The importance of paying attention to our own thoughts and actively changing the negative ones so we can truly achieve what we're capable of.

Activities

Activity 1: Belief Flip Exercise

Objective

Identify and challenge limiting beliefs by reframing them into empowering ones.

Step 1: Identify the Limiting Belief

Write down a specific limiting belief you have about yourself.

Example: *"I'm not good enough to achieve my goals."*

Step 2: Evidence Examination

List evidence that supports this belief.

Example: *"I failed a project at work."*

Step 3: Contradictory Evidence

List evidence that contradicts this belief.

Example: *"I successfully completed several projects in the past."*

Step 4: Reframe the Belief

Transform the limiting belief into a more empowering one.

Example: *"I am capable of achieving my goals with the right effort and mindset."*

Step 5: Affirmation Creation

Create a positive affirmation based on the new belief.

Example: *"I am capable and can achieve my goals."*

Reflection: Reflect on how this new belief makes you feel compared to the old one. Write down any changes in your mindset or emotions.

Activity 2: Positive Affirmation Replacement

Objective

Replace negative self-talk with positive affirmations, fostering a more optimistic mindset.

Stop speaking to yourself so negatively. Every time you catch yourself saying something negative, tell yourself three positive things instead.

Activity 3: The Five Whys

Objective

Identify and understand the root cause of a limiting belief in order to effectively address and overcome it.

Take one of your limiting beliefs and ask yourself "Why do I believe this?" Write down the answer, then ask "Why?" again, in response to that answer. Repeat this process five times to get to the root cause of your belief. Understanding the deeper reason behind a limiting belief can help you address it more effectively.

Journal Prompt

Think about a limiting belief you've held about yourself. Write a before and after story showing how this belief has limited you and how changing it will (or has) set you free.

4

A Sprinkle of Courage

RED:
A bold and powerful color, red embodies the strength and bravery inherent in courage.

I don't know about you, but I don't enjoy the feeling of being scared. I never liked playing hide and seek because I was terrified the person hiding would jump out at me and scream "Boo!" when I didn't expect it. I stayed home, pretending to not feel well, when my friends visited haunted houses on Halloween. I was afraid of opening my closet door, thinking there might be someone hiding. And you can forget about looking under my bed. Terrifying!

I don't like amusement parks, scary movies, or walking my dog alone at night. I would never jump off the high diving board, try skiing, or break the rules. As I got older, I was petrified of going to a job interview, asking a question if I didn't understand something, or quitting a job. I feared appearing dumb or not living up to expectations. Somehow, I was able to get a full-time job as an accountant at a small accounting firm after graduating college. It took months before I was comfortable and secure enough to speak up.

I worked with the same firm for ten years, even though I knew there was really no room for advancement, because I was afraid to leave. I didn't want to go through the uncomfortable process of switching jobs. It was much easier to stick with what and who I knew. I convinced myself it was good enough. Have you ever done that? Deep down, you know it would be better for you to take a chance and go out on a limb, but you lie to yourself. You try to convince yourself that the status quo is better.

I stayed at this firm until my close friend, Mary, intervened. She gave me the opportunity to move from Long Island to New Jersey and open up my own insurance agency for a large company. She was a local manager for the company, and she had an opening. I knew absolutely nothing about insurance or selling; just the idea of being a salesperson made me nauseous. Mary was a great salesperson because she explained how Gary and I could work there together. His background was sales, and mine was business, so we made a great team.

Of course, she really sold the benefits to me, like being your own boss and having freedom. After ten years of tax season, it sounded like a dream. My curiosity was piqued. *Maybe this was my ticket out. Gary could do all the selling, and I'll be behind the scenes figuring out the operations part. The worst thing that could happen if it doesn't work out is that we go back to doing what we did before.* I knew I wanted to give it a try, but I needed Gary and Mary to give me that push.

The story does eventually have a happy ending, but it took several years to get there. In the beginning, it was an absolute nightmare. I found myself in one agonizing experience after another. I dreamt of going back to the safety and familiarity of being a CPA. Each morning, when I awoke and realized I had to face another day at my insurance agency, the tears would stream down my face. All I wanted was to go home, but I knew I couldn't.

Mary had put her neck on the line for me, so I had to go on. I gained fifty pounds in two years due to all the stress eating I did. My new marriage suffered; we were broke and living in Mary's basement, and I had no time for anything other than work. I was constantly scared. I was scared that I would fail. I was scared that I would do something wrong and get fired. I was scared to speak to customers because I really didn't know what I was talking about. I was scared customers would yell at me. With all these fears running through my brain, I was scared, but I did it anyway.

As the weeks and months passed, it became easier and some of my fears subsided. I had some small victories that helped me along the way and gave me the courage to keep going. On my two-year anniversary, my probation period ended, and I breathed a huge sigh of relief because I knew I was going to make it. I had no idea how I had gotten through it, but I had. Reflecting back now, this was one of the greatest game-changers of my life.

Running my own agency allowed Gary and me to have the flexibility and freedom to do whatever we needed to in our personal lives. We dealt with infertility struggles, raising our children, the special needs of our oldest son, and taking care of my dad without worrying about taking time off. Of course, we had to build a team and a business to do all of this, but if we had stayed in our original jobs, it would have been out of our control.

What else have I missed out on because I lacked courage?

Our fear often comes from our limiting beliefs. I thought I wasn't good enough. I didn't want to be judged or rejected. I wasn't worthy.

> **Our fear often comes from our limiting beliefs. I thought I wasn't good enough. I didn't want to be judged or rejected. I wasn't worthy. Those beliefs created a fear of trying something new.**

Those beliefs created a fear of trying something new. Without them, I would've jumped at the opportunity. I don't know if anyone is able to get rid of those thoughts completely, but we can learn how to overcome them, beginning with the strategies mentioned in the last chapter.

But here's the thing: the fear will never go away completely. We have to acknowledge that fear and continue to move forward. Oh, is that all? You might be thinking, "I get it, but it is so damn hard." However, each time you face that fear, you're growing. You're proving to yourself that you can do it. You're building your confidence muscle. Even if it doesn't work out, you are still a success because you tried and learned something from your experience.

Pause for a moment and think about a time when you were petrified about something but still did it. What was the outcome? How did it make you feel? Would you do it again?

If you have a growth mindset, then failure is encouraged because it teaches us something. I don't know about you, but in reflecting on my life, I see how each time I faced my fears, I benefited from the experience. Although it wasn't necessarily fun to live through, in the end, I see how it gave me some type of gift, usually in the form of increased confidence or courage.

You might not realize it, but each day you are doing something that takes courage.

It takes courage to turn down an invitation.
It takes courage to speak up about something.
It takes courage to say I'm sorry.
It takes courage to help others.
It takes courage to keep your commitments.
It takes courage to ask for help.
It takes courage to do the right thing.

Most likely, you don't even realize what you're doing, but each of these seemingly small actions adds up.

> **You have what it takes to stand up to those fears. You're already doing it in small, simple acts.**

You have what it takes to stand up to those fears. You're already doing it in small, simple acts.

You picked up this book because you're ready for a change, whether it's a major transformation or a small shift. But remember, change requires stepping out of your comfort zone. It's tempting to stick to what's familiar and easy, but that comfort can keep you from truly living and growing. Staying comfortable means missing out on opportunities to expand your horizons and reach your full potential. I'm not willing to settle for that, and I know you aren't either. Embrace the discomfort and open yourself up to new possibilities.

Each time you face that fear, you're growing. You're proving to yourself that you can do it. You're building your confidence muscle.

Key Takeaways:

1. Fear Is Natural; Courage Is a Choice: Embrace fear as a part of life, but recognize that stepping beyond it to pursue new opportunities is where true growth and transformation happen.

2. Small Acts of Courage Build Confidence: Regularly facing fears, even in small ways, strengthens your confidence and proves to yourself that you can handle challenges.

3. Growth Through Discomfort: Stepping out of your comfort zone is essential for personal development and achieving your full potential.

Activities

Activity 1: The Courage Challenge

Objective

Perform an act of courage that confronts a small fear.

Instructions:

1. Identify a fear you face in daily life that you usually avoid, such as speaking up in meetings or trying a new activity.

2. Challenge yourself to confront this fear within the next week. Plan how and when you'll do it.

3. After completing the challenge, reflect on the experience and how it made you feel to step outside your comfort zone.

Activity 2: New Experience Explorer

Objective

Try something completely new to you.

Instructions:

1. Choose an activity you've never done before but have thought about trying—anything from a cooking class to starting a simple exercise routine.

2. Commit to trying this new activity at least once in the next two weeks.

3. Write about the experience: What did you do? How did it feel before, during, and after?

Activity 3: Facing Fears with Courage

Objective

Create a plan for facing fears with actionable steps.

Instructions:

1. Draw a grid with two columns: fear and actionable steps.

2. List your fears in the first column and corresponding actions you can take to face them in the second column.

3. Choose one action to focus on in the coming month.

Journal Prompt

Write about a moment when you felt intense fear but decided to face it anyway. What was the situation, and what motivated you to take that step?

5

A Sprinkle of Responsibility

GREEN:
The color of growth and vitality, green suits the nurturing and sustaining nature of responsibility.

I was under the impression that my life unfolded as it was supposed to, and there was nothing I could do about it. Now, obviously, I knew I had made certain decisions that led me down different paths, but once I was there and events outside my control happened, I felt stuck. I resigned myself to the fact that this is just the way it is. I wondered, *Why do other people seem to have an easier life than I do? Why was my life so fraught with challenges and struggles compared to my friends and family?*

The bottom line, even though I hate to admit it, is that I felt sorry for myself. Of course, I knew I was very lucky in so many ways, but that's not where I decided to place my focus. I searched for validation to support my hypothesis that my life was tougher than others. Every time something happened, I added it to my bag of proof. Others would also help by telling me that it was incredible how my life seemed to be one challenge after another. I would make sure to drop those nuggets in my pity bag as well.

I went on like that for years, doing what needed to be done each day, checking off my tasks, and searching for proof that I was correct in thinking that I had it rough. This continued until I was introduced to a simple formula that changed my life. The formula comes from the book *The Success Principles*, written by Jack Canfield and Janet Switzer:

$$E + R = O$$
Event + Response = Outcome

Simply put, when an event occurs, you respond to it, which determines the outcome. Let me give you an example. I wake up in the morning, and it's raining. I grab an umbrella and walk out the door to head off to work. I arrive at my office, dry and ready to start my day. If my response was to ignore the rain and walk to work without an umbrella, I would have arrived soaked and, in turn, uncomfortable and miserable. The event was the same in both cases—it was raining. How I chose to respond changed the outcome.

POW!!!

I was under the impression that the formula was Event = Outcome.

I didn't understand that the event wasn't the only thing that determined the outcome. In my mind, there was no R, or the R was irrelevant. What a revelation! By not acknowledging the R, I blamed everything and everyone else, taking zero responsibility for the outcome. On a surface level, it's easier to do that than to own up to the fact

If you don't like the outcome, and the opportunity exists to change your response, why not give it a try and see what happens?

that I made mistakes along the way that led to outcomes I was not pleased with.

If you don't like the outcome and the opportunity exists to change your response, why not give it a try and see what happens?

I had the power to change my life, one response at a time, and I never knew it. I found this

> **I had the power to change my life, one response at a time, and I never knew it.**

new knowledge to be extremely empowering. I was embarrassed that I blamed everyone and everything else, but I realized how lucky I was to have figured it out. I was excited to experiment and put the formula to the test.

I mentioned earlier that I had some serious money problems. Applying E + R = O to money led to some tough realizations. Growing up, money was an area of great stress in our lives. We never had enough money, yet my parents wanted to live a life that was beyond our means, so they used credit cards to acquire possessions and go on vacations. I'm not talking about anything extravagant at all. It was the difference between being middle-class and upper-middle-class.

Once or twice a month, on a Saturday or Sunday afternoon, my father would sit down at his small wooden desk in the corner of our living room and pay the bills. I didn't know the specifics of what he was doing or how difficult it was, but I knew it made him turn into a red-faced stress monster. We all knew not to upset him, doing our best to stay out of his way for the rest of the day. He would sit at the desk, grumbling and cursing to himself as his shoulders stiffened. I'd see him sitting there with his head down, held up by his hands as they covered his face.

We would often hear the common phrases "Money doesn't grow on trees" or "Do you think I'm made of money?" I would sometimes hear my parents argue about purchasing a new car or piece of furniture. It wasn't an argument regarding which car or couch to buy, but instead an argument over whether or not they could afford it.

Watching and listening to them instilled some core beliefs around money for me: money = stress.

For me, money was unattainable.

Once I lived on my own, I fell into the same patterns my parents taught me. I bought a new car and had a large car payment. I had several credit cards that I used to purchase things I needed or wanted. The next thing I knew, I was hunched over my desk (although black Formica, not wooden) trying to figure out how I could possibly pay these bills with the salary I made.

When I got engaged, I had to come clean and share my money situation with Gary. I had over ten thousand dollars in credit card debt, a car loan, and zero dollars in a savings or retirement account. Gary was shocked when he heard my confession. He had assumed, since I was a CPA, that I would have had my financial affairs in order. He needed a few days to digest this information, and I was afraid he would change his mind regarding our impending nuptials.

Thankfully, that didn't happen, and we were married on May 8, 1994. We used part of our wedding money to pay for our honeymoon, planning to use the remainder to pay down my debt. However, we soon needed the money to finance our move from Long Island to New Jersey to open up our insurance agency.

Just like most things in life, the expenses were much higher than anticipated, and the debt kept piling up, but we kept telling ourselves that in the end it would pay off. After a few years, that is exactly what happened, and it was the most incredible feeling! For the first time in my adult life, I had no debt other than car payments and actually had money to spend and save. It was exhilarating and life-changing to no longer worry about how I would pay my bills.

It was the perfect time to buy our forever home. We wound up going with a new build and didn't take into consideration that window treatments, paint (other than builder's paint), and landscaping were not included. We also put in a few more upgrades than we initially thought, and the price jumped up. We moved from an apartment into a four-bedroom house that we now had to furnish. The money flew out faster than it came in, but we still avoided the debt trap. However, this exhilarating freedom quickly dissipated.

A year later, the bottom fell out of the auto insurance market, and with it went our income. Our income dropped by twenty percent at the same time we incurred extremely high medical bills for the many in vitro fertilization procedures we had. We started using our credit cards again without being able to pay them in full each month.

When our oldest son Sam was diagnosed with autism spectrum disorder, I wanted to do anything and everything to help him. I hired a team of therapists to work with him for twenty to thirty hours per week, and none of it was covered by insurance. For several years, we spent an average of six thousand dollars per month on therapists and treatments. We did not have the money, so we took out a home equity line of credit and watched the balance increase month after month.

As he got older, those costs decreased but there always seemed to be something. Our income never recovered from that twenty percent hit, and we continued in the same fashion my parents had years earlier. As time went on and I could no longer figure it out, I began putting off paying our estimated taxes to the IRS each quarter. Although I was late, I'd eventually pay them; however, this meant also paying interest and penalties.

My payments grew later and later until I was a couple of years behind. At that point, Gary suffered from serious anxiety and depression, so I couldn't share the situation with him. I forced myself not to think about it because it scared the heck out of me and made me sick to my stomach. I saw no way out, and if I even attempted to suggest that we watch our spending, Gary slipped into depression. I couldn't take that, so I went on silently suffering.

I tried not to think about it because the moment I did, I felt terror, shame, and anxiety slowly build inside of me until I'd find myself trembling internally. *How would I ever get us out of this mess? How did I let this happen in the first place? I should have taken control years ago. Now, it's too late.* I would try to push these thoughts out of my head, concentrating on something else.

In February 2020, Oprah toured the country in conjunction with Weight Watchers. She visited various cities, holding day-long motivational events in big arenas where she'd have a different celebrity guest. In Brooklyn, Michelle Obama was the guest, and I was not missing the opportunity to see Oprah and Michelle.

My cousin Mindy and I spent an inspirational day listening to speakers, dancing in our seats, and filling out our workbooks as Oprah instructed us. At the end of the day, Oprah took the stage alone, sharing a very vulnerable story with the audience. Even though there were sixteen thousand other people in the arena, it felt very intimate. She said that all of us, at one time or another, have had a secret eating away at us—a secret we don't want to think about or deal with. Tears streamed down my face as she spoke. *How did she know? How did she know my money secret?*

She then explained how if we keep that secret inside, eating away at us, it will eventually explode like a volcano, and we will have no control over what happens. Instead, we need to allow that secret to come to the surface and address it. She told us it might not be an easy thing to do, and it could be tough and get messy, but that's okay. In the end, we would have control, no longer bearing the burden. Acknowledging it and dealing with it would set us free.

As I let her message sink in, I knew she was right. Nothing good would happen if I continued to ignore this problem. Wiping away the tears, I vowed that I would take her advice and come up with a strategy to get out of this mess.

The minute I took action, I felt like a different person. There was no quick or easy way out of this situation, and some of the steps I took were painful. I carried so much shame that having to share my story with bankruptcy and tax attorneys made me feel like a failure and a loser. However, I reminded myself that everyone makes mistakes, and I was now, *finally*, taking one-hundred percent responsibility. All the excuses I told myself for years were lies to make myself feel better, but, in the end, they delayed the inevitable.

You see, it's easy to get down on yourself for making mistakes, big or small. It's crushing when we are honest with ourselves and take responsibility for decisions we made that got us into the mess. However, let's think about this another way: once we truly own it, we have the power to get ourselves out of it too. We don't need to rely on anyone else; it's all us. Sure, we need others' help, and we can't control certain things, but we can always control how we react to them. This is the secret sauce—the power that each of us possess—and when we embrace our power, we transform ourselves.

Did my financial mess resolve quickly? Absolutely not. I'm still dealing with it several years later. Did I have challenges and roadblocks along the way? Hell yes! Sometimes it felt like one after the other, but each boulder left me with a choice. There's always a choice of how to react to those boulders, regardless of how big, scary, or awful they might be.

Once we truly own it, we have the power to get ourselves out of it too. We don't need to rely on anyone else; it's all us.

Think about it for a minute. Why is it that there are so many who suffer terrible losses, trauma, and poverty yet still manage to turn their lives around while others wind up angry, poor, and hopeless? What's the difference between them? The difference is simple: it's what they thought. The first group took responsibility for their situation, making choices to go around or through roadblocks to build the life they wanted, while the second group stopped, thinking there was no way out.

Let's think about the formula: $E + R = O$. Assuming the events (E) were similar in each group, they each had different outcomes (O) because of their different responses (R). If you are not happy with the outcome and have no control over the event, the one thing you have control over and can change is your response. We can apply this to pretty much everything. Our life's path is made up of the responses or choices we make along the way.

It's so simple yet incredibly powerful. Once you truly understand it, it becomes exciting because every day we have at least a few pebbles thrown in front of us, and we decide how we will react to them. On average, we make 35,000 choices a day. *What should I wear? What should I eat? Should I work on that now or later? Should I ask my boss this question, or will I sound dumb?* These are just a few examples. Think how your life would be different today if you had made different choices in the past.

Now, I'm not telling you to think about this so you'll berate yourself for choices you made that led to poor outcomes; in fact, it's the opposite. Forgive yourself, but then realize that the choices you make today, right now, will determine your future. You're clearly making an excellent choice already by reading this book! Now, your next choice is whether or not you'll complete the activities in this chapter. If you do take the time and are honest with yourself (I mean, really, really honest), your future self will thank you.

> **Key Takeaways:**
>
> 1. Control Your Response: The formula Event + Response = Outcome shows us that our power lies in how we respond, not in what happens to us. By focusing on our reactions, we can truly influence the results.
>
> 2. Stepping Up to the Plate: Realizing that you have a hand in the outcomes of your life through how you respond to events is crucial. It's about owning up to the fact that you're not a passive observer but an active participant in your story.
>
> 3. Owning Your Choices: Taking responsibility means recognizing that you hold the steering wheel in your life's journey. This realization is empowering, giving you the freedom to navigate life's ups and downs with confidence and purpose.

Activities

Activity 1: The E+R=O Experiment

Objective

Apply the E+R=O formula to a recent event and analyze the outcome.

Instructions:

1. Think of a recent situation where you were unhappy with the outcome.

2. Write down the event (E), your response (R), and the outcome (O) as it happened.

3. Now, brainstorm alternative responses (R) you could have chosen. Write down how each alternative would have potentially changed the outcome (O).

4. Reflect on this exercise's insights and how you might apply this awareness to future events.

Activity 2: Choice Mapping

Objective

Visualize how different choices lead to different paths.

Materials Needed:

- Large paper
- Colored pens or markers

Instructions:

1. At the center of the paper, write down a choice you're facing.

2. Draw branches out from the center, each one representing a possible decision you can make.

3. For each branch, branch out further to show possible outcomes of each decision.

4. Reflect on this map to see how varied your life's path can be based on the choices you make.

Activity 3: Small Changes, Big Impact

Objective

Compile a list of small changes you can make that can lead to significant improvements in your life.

Instructions:

1. List five small changes you can implement today or this week.

2. Next to each, note the impact or outcome you hope to see from making this change.

3. At the end of the week or month, review this list and note any progress or insights gained.

Journal Prompt

Write about a situation you need to forgive yourself for regarding a past decision. How can taking responsibility for your future choices help you move on?

6

A Sprinkle of Dreams

PURPLE:
Often associated with imagination, inspiration, and spirituality, purple evokes a sense of mystery and wonder.

Do you know how to dream? I don't mean when you're sleeping, but when you're awake. As a little girl, my dreams were fairly realistic—nothing too over the top. I wanted to be married at age twenty-seven and, two years later, have my first child (preferably a son), and then a daughter would complete my family in another couple of years. I would be a teacher, and my handsome, loving husband would be some type of professional. We would live in a lovely neighborhood in a four-bedroom house. This was my happily ever after.

As I grew to be an adult, my dreams expanded to include being a lottery winner. I desperately longed for financial freedom but assumed that luck was the only way this goal could be achieved. My dreams never aimed higher. Other than the lottery, they were very realistic and within reach. I didn't allow myself to dream any bigger, possibly to protect myself from disappointment when they didn't come true.

> **What a mistake I was making by limiting myself. I limited the possibilities of what might be attainable if I only believed in myself and my ability to make my dreams come true.**

What a mistake I was making by limiting myself. I limited the possibilities of what might be attainable if I only believed in myself and my ability to make my dreams come true. This was really the root of the problem. I didn't believe in myself. I could list all the reasons why the dreams I didn't dare to dream would never happen. What I didn't know then, but I do now, is that, of course, they would never happen because I believed they never would.

Remember: change your thoughts, change your life.

As I began the first personal development course with Elizabeth, the first exercise I was given was to write, in detail, about my dream life. What would the details of a day look like? Where would I live? What would I wear? What would I eat? Who would I be with?

I was stumped. I had absolutely no idea. I never allowed myself to even consider such a thing. For weeks, I struggled to dig deep down and be honest with myself. I tried to put myself into this dream and try it on for size to see if I liked what my mind created. I then took my pen to paper and wrote it out. Here is my very first attempt at describing my dream life, completely unedited:

My new company will grow into a multi-million-dollar business that will help thousands of people regain their lives and sanity by reminding and teaching them to take care of themselves. I will be on the board of directors, and the boys will be running the company if they choose. If not, I will hire a CEO so I can semi-retire.

Every day I will wake up in my beautiful bedroom and be smiling just thinking about the day ahead. I will do yoga, meditate, journal, and eat a healthy breakfast. I'll then get ready to go to an exercise class or play pickleball with friends. In the afternoon, I'll work for a few hours and then enjoy the afternoon and evening with my loving, adoring partner.

He will be someone who is positive and believes that anything is possible. He will be a source of light and energy, someone who can make me laugh, and is good company. In the evening, we will watch a show or read a book. I will be a reader.

Sometimes we'll go out with friends in the evening, and other nights we'll enjoy a quiet evening. We'll enjoy and appreciate the sunshine and our beautiful surroundings. I will see Sam and Ben as often as possible. I will be a big part of my grandchildren's lives. I'll be there to watch their games, recitals, etc. They will know just how much I love them and that I will always be there for them.

My life will be filled with love, joy, and happiness. I will appreciate the gift of every day and make the most of it.

I will travel several times a year to Europe, different parts of the United States, or a tropical location. I will travel with my partner, friends, or family. We will fly first class and stay in beautiful hotels with wonderful service. We will have the VIP package and get to see all the sights of our destination.

I will live a long and happy life. I will eat a healthy diet and make exercise a daily priority. I will enjoy massages and facials whenever I like.

I will have abundant financial wealth that will allow me to enjoy the finer things in life. I will have a home in Florida, one in Rehoboth Beach, and another wherever the kids live. Each home will be beautifully decorated with the help of a decorator. I will be able to pay for my grandchildren's education and have enough money to leave it to my family, so they won't have to worry.

That's as far as I got, but not bad for a first attempt. It was difficult because, even though I wanted all the things I wrote about and more, it was hard to believe it could ever happen. And therein lies the problem. If you don't believe it's possible, then it's not. Is someone going to come in with a magic wand and make it all happen? Nope. It won't be easy, and it will take hard work, dedication, and perseverance, but if this is what I wanted my life to look like, then I needed to get started right away.

If you don't believe it's possible, then it's not.

We were instructed to read what we wrote at least once a day and, even more importantly, to close our eyes and visualize that dream, noticing how we felt. A funny thing happened as day after day I followed the instructions. I started to believe it was possible. It was up to me to figure out how to get there, which we'll talk about later, but now I knew where I wanted to go.

Things started to come together for me. It made sense that I needed to know where I'm going in order to figure out how to get there. If you don't know your destination, what are the chances you'll ever find it? I knew where I was now and where I wanted to go, and now I had to figure out how to get from A to B. Simple, right?

Nope.

It's not simple. There will always be forks in the road, and you are probably going to pick the wrong fork, but that's okay as long as you're able to learn from your mistakes and course-correct. I decided that I had nothing to lose. It felt good to have a direction and a goal. Now, I just had to figure out my strategy.

Overwhelmed as I contemplated my first step, I found myself thinking about a friend of mine, Christine. Chris is a four-foot-eleven, ninety-pound force of nature. We met when our kids were in preschool, and I can still remember my first impressions of her. First, it was her size. At that point, I was at one of my higher weights—at five-foot-six and a weight I will not disclose, we looked ridiculous standing next to each other.

Based on her appearance, I thought she would be quiet and demure, but boy was I wrong. This woman was and is a powerhouse; her mental toughness is evident in all she sets out to accomplish. She was a gymnast and a cheerleader growing up, but as she got ready to finish high school and leave home to attend college, her life was forever changed.

She was teaching a gymnastics class and demonstrated a basic move that she had done hundreds of times, but this time something went wrong and she broke her back. She was paralyzed and told she would never walk again. She was unable to go to college as planned, but once the shock wore off, Chris was determined to walk again.

She didn't listen to any doctor or therapist. She worked tirelessly, dealing with pain and disappointment as if she were immortal. In the end, she defied the odds and was able to walk again with a slight limp. She went on to go to college the following year, living the life she envisioned for herself.

Even now, there are days when she's in great pain and can't get out of bed. Her husband needs to pick her up and carry her to the bathroom because her back spasms are so bad. Yet in all the years we've known each other, I have never heard her complain. It's the opposite. This woman knows what she wants for herself and her family, and each decision she makes is intentional based on her desires.

Chris doesn't care about being liked. She speaks her mind without worrying about what others think. I have been the opposite, always worrying about others' opinions of me. I've watched in amazement over the past twenty years as Chris has stood up to school administrators, teachers, and coaches. As her mom's caregiver, she did the same with doctors, therapists, and nursing home personnel. She has never let anything or anyone stop her from reaching her own goals for herself and her family.

Imagine if she gave in, believing there was nothing she could do to help herself at the age of eighteen. She was determined and focused on her destination, which was to be able to walk again, and she was going to figure it out one way or another, regardless of other opinions.

She is unstoppable, and you can be the same. Think about your own dreams. Like my friend Christine, you've got what it takes to face big challenges and push through. It's not about the curveballs life throws at us; it's how we swing at them that really counts. Dream a lot. Let yourself fantasize about what could be, and then believe it can actually happen. Take it from me: a sprinkle of dreams can take you places you've never imagined. Go ahead, set your sights high, start small if you have to, and let's chase those dreams together. Here's to making the unbelievable believable!

Key Takeaways:

1. **Let Yourself Dream:** Don't hold back—imagine the biggest, boldest life you can. Believing in your dreams is the first step to making them come true.

2. **Your Attitude Matters:** How you react to what life throws at you shapes where you end up. Stay positive and see challenges as opportunities to grow.

3. **Act on Your Dreams:** Hope isn't just wishful thinking; it's a call to action. Start small, keep at it, and those big dreams will start to feel a lot closer.

Dream a lot. Let yourself fantasize about what could be, and then believe it can actually happen. Take it from me: a sprinkle of dreams can take you places you've never imagined.

Activities

Activity 1: Dream Visualization

Objective

Vividly visualize and connect with your dream life.

Instructions:

1. Find a quiet space where you won't be disturbed.

2. Close your eyes and imagine your dream life in as much detail as possible, using the prompts from the chapter as a guide. Focus on how this life feels, the sounds around you, the people you're with, and what a typical day looks like.

3. Afterwards, write about the experience, highlighting the emotions and sensations you felt.

Activity 2: I Can Achieve My Dreams Because...

Objective

Build confidence in your ability to achieve your dreams.

Instructions:

1. List reasons why you are capable of achieving your dreams, focusing on your strengths, past successes, and resources.

2. Add to this list whenever you accomplish something that reinforces your belief in yourself.

Activity 3: Dreams vs. Limiting Beliefs

Objective

Identify and counteract the limiting beliefs holding you back from your dreams.

Materials Needed:

- Paper
- Pens
- Or, a digital note-taking app

Instructions:

1. Draw a two-column grid. In the first column, write down your dreams. In the second column, list out the limiting beliefs associated with each dream.

2. For each limiting belief, write a counterstatement that challenges and reframes the belief into something positive and empowering.

Journal Prompt

Reflect on a dream that you've previously set aside as unrealistic or unattainable. What is one small step you could take today that might bring you closer to making this dream a reality? Write about how achieving this dream could transform your life.

7

A Sprinkle of Direction

ORANGE:
Vibrant and energetic, orange signifies movement and direction with purpose.

At this point, you have taken responsibility for your life. You can picture that dream life of yours just waiting for you, and you can't wait to get there. But how? Just dreaming and believing isn't enough. It's going to take getting messy, failing, stopping, and starting again, but it will all be well worth it.

When you picture your life now versus your dream life, it can feel overwhelming and impossible, so we need to start by breaking it down into manageable pieces. The first step is to assess the different areas of your life, determining your overall satisfaction in each by assigning a number on a scale of one to ten. You will determine the categories, but here are some examples: career, finances, spirituality, health, physical environment, significant other, friends and family, fun, and personal growth. You can add, subtract, or rename them. It's your life, no one else's.

Now, repeat the same process while visualizing your dream life. Assign a number for each category based on where you feel you'd be once your dreams are reality. On first glance, you may think that each one needs to be a ten, but that isn't necessarily true. Then, subtract your current number from your dream life number to see how far apart they are. Now, since I'm a numbers gal, I like to look at the visual representation of the numbers. You can make it as simple or complicated as you like. You can do it on your computer and design a beautiful chart, but here's what works for me:

Category	Current	Dream	Needed
Career	6	9	3
Finances	4	10	6
Spirituality	7	9	2
Health	5	8	3
Physical Environment	7	10	3
Significant Other	2	8	6
Friends & Family	8	9	1
Fun	8	9	1
Personal Growth	9	9	0

In this example, you can see that finances and significant other are the two categories where the most growth is needed in order to reach my dream life. However, the majority of others require some work as well. With this information, we can now set goals in each category. Now, there are a gazillion books written about how to set goals, so if you already have a method that works for you, fantastic! If not, I want to make this as easy as possible for you. I don't want you to overthink it.

I want you to set one goal for yourself in all the categories that need improvement. In my example, it would be all but one. Make sure they are S.M.A.R.T. goals:

Specific

Measurable

Achievable

Relevant

Time-bound

Let me give you a few examples. Let's create a financial goal since I need to jump from a four to a ten in that category.

Example 1: I will own a home by the beach.

This is a lovely goal, but it's not S.M.A.R.T.

Example 2: I will own a 2,500-square-foot home in Rehoboth Beach, DE, by May 1, 2027.

Do you see the difference? Let's try another.

Example 1: I will have enough money to pay off all my debt.

Example 2: I will have paid my debts of one hundred thousand dollars in full by January 1, 2026.

Get the idea? You can write one or more goals in each of the categories. It's up to you. Having too many goals doesn't mean that you need to overwhelm yourself and work on all of them simultaneously. I suggest picking a couple to focus on at a time. You could consider working on a few goals in different areas of your life—maybe try a career goal and a personal goal.

In the example above, you could choose a financial and relationship goal or a career and physical environment goal. Perhaps you want to work on two relationship goals, one with your partner and the other with your friends. Remember, if whatever you choose isn't working for you, you can change it.

So, let's assume one of the goals you chose was to pay off one hundred thousand dollars of debt by January 1, 2026. You might be thinking, "That's a great goal, but how the heck am I possibly going to do that?" At least that's what I was thinking when I made a similar goal a few years ago. It felt impossible, so I found I needed to break it down into smaller, more manageable steps while still keeping the bigger goal in mind.

I learned firsthand about the importance of goal-setting in my twenties. After graduating from college, I began my public accounting career. In order to progress in accounting, I needed to get my certification and become a CPA (Certified Public Accountant). Back then, we were told that the CPA exam made the bar exam (to become a lawyer) look like a kindergarten test. There were four separate parts to the test, which were taken separately. Rarely did someone take all four at the same time; however, there was one catch. You had to take at least two together and pass them both the first time. After that, you could take the other two individually.

Now, just to be clear, each test requires several months of studying. I was a great student in elementary school, a good student in high school, and an average student in college. Why did it change, you ask? I was lazy. I never had to study very hard, so I didn't develop good habits. As the work became harder, my A-plus grades downgraded to an A and then a B and occasionally lower.

I knew I needed to really study for the exam, but I had no plan. My goal was to pass the test. I had no idea how I would accomplish the goal other than, obviously, studying. So I studied a little more than I had in college, but as the test date drew near, I didn't have a full understanding of all the material. Even though I hadn't been a straight-A student in college, I had never failed a test, so why should this time be different? Hopefully, the exam would be heavily weighted towards the topics I was confident in.

The two parts I chose to take together were given over the weekend. My test site was in a not-very-nice neighborhood in Jamaica, Queens. Traveling to an unfamiliar, somewhat unsafe area heightened the sense of dread I felt the night before the first part. As I sat at my desk with pencil and paper in hand (this was 1987), reading questions that could be interpreted in a number of different ways, panic set in.

What if I fail? What will everyone think? That I'm dumb? What about my employer? Will they fire me? What a jerk I was! How had I not devoted more time to this?

After it was over, I thought it was possible that I might have passed. The hardest part was the waiting. It took two months to get the test results in the mail. Initially, I tried to calculate the percentage of questions I answered correctly, which is next to impossible, especially for an exam of this complexity and length. I then imagined what it would feel like to pass or fail. As the weeks went on, I would rush to the mailbox, sifting through the letters, wanting the torture to end.

What do you think happened? Pass or fail? Actually, both answers are correct. I passed one part and failed the other part by one point. This meant that even the part I passed did not count and would need to be retaken. My worst nightmare!

I had certainly failed at things over the years, but nothing of this magnitude. I was embarrassed and ashamed because I knew if I had devoted the amount of time necessary, I would have passed. I did this to myself. After the tough job of telling everyone the news, I knew it was time to get serious. Passing this beast of a test wouldn't happen by wishing and making a half-assed attempt. I needed to devise a goal and a plan. I was determined to not let this happen again.

I bit the bullet and signed up for a review course that met all day on Saturday for months (again, 1987, so online didn't exist). I hated the idea, but I knew I had no choice. I vowed to attend each class and keep up with the studying as outlined in the course, which meant I needed to allocate several weeknights and Sundays to it. I kept telling myself that in the scope of my life, this was nothing, but it sure didn't feel like nothing as the weeks rolled on.

Back to Jamaica I went, and I was even more fearful. Failing once was bad enough, but the idea of failing again was unbearable. I tried to keep those negative thoughts out of my mind and concentrate on the exam, question by question. Even though I was more confident this time, I still had no idea of the outcome.

As I opened the letter from the State of New York, tears of relief and pride immediately sprung from my eyes as a loud scream escaped my mouth. I had done it! Goal accomplished! Two more parts to go, but now I knew there was no stopping me.

The Sprinkle Effect

On April 24, 1989, I reached my goal and became a certified public accountant.

The difference between passing and failing was having mini-goals and strategies along the way. The course I took provided me with mini-goals, but I personalized them by assigning due dates to each of the modules. Every day, it was crystal clear what I needed to accomplish. It took away the guesswork and provided me with a small victory each time I completed the assigned task.

> **The difference between passing and failing was having mini-goals and strategies along the way.**

Once you have your big goals, you need to drill down and identify the actions you will need to take in order to move forward. It's often helpful to create mini goals along the way. Those smaller goals should be much less intimidating and feel more realistic to achieve.

I first applied this strategy to tackling my lifelong weight problem. I have been on so many different diets over the years that I can't begin to count. Most of the time, I had to lose fifty or more pounds, which felt impossible and like it would take forever. Sometimes, I would last only a couple of weeks because the diets were too restrictive or forced me to eat food I didn't like, and other times, I would stick with them for a few months and lose twenty-five pounds or so. The minute I "cheated," I found it nearly impossible to get back on the diet, so I went back to my old habits. Thinking about how far I still was from my goal made me feel defeated.

Sound familiar?

This pattern has unsuccessfully been followed by many of us, regardless of whether or not the issue is weight. I would set a goal that felt unattainable, and after a few months, I would get frustrated and tell myself I would never reach my goal. The tongue lashing I gave to myself were reminders of all the things that were wrong with me: undisciplined, no willpower, lazy, and a pig, just to name a few. I would never dream of speaking to another person the way I spoke to myself.

After forty years of dealing with the losing, never reaching my goal, gaining, and berating cycle, I decided it was time to try something different. As Albert Einstein once said, "Insanity is doing the same thing over and over and expecting different results." Each time that I tried to lose weight, I had a perfectionist mindset. Either I was on a diet or off. If I went off, it was over. I would set goals for myself, such as losing twenty-five pounds in three months. If I didn't achieve or come close to the goal, I was defeated. Game over.

It was clearly time to approach this differently, so instead of focusing on the one hundred pounds I needed to lose, I set a much smaller goal. I was going to go back to Weight Watchers yet again, and my goal was to attend the meeting each week. I had no expectations around eating, exercising, or tracking my food. I had no expectations about how much weight I should lose or in what timeframe. I didn't care. My only goal was to show up every week for the meeting.

And that's exactly what I did for three months–I just showed up. I lost a couple of pounds, which, for someone who needed to lose one hundred pounds, was nothing.

Once I created this new habit of attending the meeting, it was time to set a new goal: I would track my food and the points value (a Weight Watchers thing) fifty percent of the time. Again, no goal around weight loss. Adding this new goal to the habit I created of attending the meetings weekly started to have an effect on my confidence level.

I was proud that I had attained my first goal and was excited to try and conquer this new one. In the past, the idea of tracking my food was irritating and something I avoided, but this time it was different. I felt empowered and didn't have the same self-imposed pressure I felt in the past. I didn't need to be perfect and record my food and points all the time; half the time was good enough. I achieved the goals I set for myself, which gave me faith that I could do this.

Tracking half the time—*check!* I increased my percentage to seventy, and it felt doable. After all, it was only increasing my goal by twenty percent. I could do that! The scale sometimes rewarded me, and other times it did not, and I was okay with that. Now let's be real here. Of course, I wanted to see the number on the scale go down each week, but I began to notice a pattern. I would lose two or three pounds one week, and then for the next two, I would go up or down a pound. In weeks three or four, I would have another bigger loss.

My goal no longer included how much weight I lost each week or how much weight I needed to lose by a certain date. I stuck to the small goals involving my habits and watched as the weight slowly began to come off. If I didn't achieve my goals of tracking or attending the meeting, I was kind to myself. I no longer beat myself up but instead said, "That's okay" and set a goal of getting back on track. Newsflash: I'm not perfect, and neither are you. None of us are, so why do we try to hold ourselves to impossible standards?

I then decided to add exercise goals and even self-care goals because I knew that I was an emotional eater. Stress eating was a favorite of mine, so if I took care of myself properly and was less stressed, then I would not be as inclined to eat to reduce stress.

I'd love to tell you that I lost one hundred pounds and have kept it off for years, but I can't. However, I did lose ninety pounds about seven years ago. It took me three years to do it, and I haven't reached that original goal yet, but it's not important anymore. I made my goal all about the number on the scale, but it turned out that wasn't as important as the behavioral changes and strong habits I developed. I am at a healthier weight, and I've learned to maintain my weight for the first time in my life. Sure, I've gained ten pounds or so, but I've caught it before that ten or fifteen pounds turned into fifty. How have I done it? I no longer create goals that make it almost impossible to achieve or make the process so unappetizing (excuse the food reference, LOL) that I quit.

What made this time different from all the others? Weight Watchers didn't change their program other than the small tweaks they make each year. The difference was all in how I approached the journey. Instead of focusing on my overall goal of losing a large amount of weight, I broke it down into small, manageable mini goals that I could achieve. I shifted my thinking, got rid of that perfectionist mentality, and stopped berating myself for not losing weight faster or for "cheating."

Now it's your turn. We've talked a lot about setting goals and finding your direction, but remember, it's all about taking those first steps. Don't get overwhelmed by the big picture. Break it down, set realistic goals, and take it one day at a time. Start small, stay consistent, and keep moving forward. Your dreams aren't just fantasies; they're a roadmap for your future.

> **Your dreams aren't just fantasies; they're a roadmap for your future.**

Don't get overwhelmed by the big picture. Break it down, set realistic goals, and take it one day at a time.

Key Takeaways:

1. Set S.M.A.R.T. Goals: Ensure your goals are specific, measurable, achievable, relevant, and time-bound to increase the likelihood of success.

2. Break It Down: Divide your ultimate goals into smaller, manageable steps to prevent feeling overwhelmed and to make progress more achievable.

3. Stay Consistent: Consistency is key in achieving goals. Start with small steps and maintain a steady effort to gradually build toward your larger aspirations.

Activities

Activity 1: Life Assessment Exercise

Objective
Identify and evaluate current satisfaction levels across various life domains, helping to pinpoint areas needing improvement and setting the stage for targeted goal setting.

Instructions:

1. List out categories that represent important areas of your life (health, career, relationships, etc.).

2. Rate your current satisfaction level in each area on a scale of one to ten.

3. Then, rate where you'd like them to be in your ideal life.

This will help you see where you want to focus your goal-setting efforts.

Activity 2: Set S.M.A.R.T. Goals

Objective
Develop clear, structured, and realistic goals for each identified area of improvement, ensuring they are S.M.A.R.T.

For each category you want to improve, set specific, measurable, achievable, relevant, and time-bound goals.

Activity 3: Create an Action Plan

Objective

Outline detailed, step-by-step actions required to achieve each S.M.A.R.T. goal, with specific timelines that foster accountability and track progress.

Break down your S.M.A.R.T. goals into smaller, actionable steps. Assign deadlines in one month, six months, and one year, up to your goal-achievement deadline, to each step to keep yourself accountable.

Journal Prompt

Think about the potential obstacles you might face in achieving your goals. For each obstacle, write down a strategy or solution to overcome it. This proactive thinking can prepare you for the challenges ahead.

8

A Sprinkle of Vision

VIOLET:
Often associated with imagination and spiritual insight, violet is perfect for vision.

Are you a daydreamer? Staring off into space, imagining what life would be like if you achieved your goals or won the lottery? Clearly, that's me, since I keep mentioning the lottery! I have a whole plan for those lottery winnings, and it's fun to picture myself helping my friends and family, buying that dream house, and traveling to places I thought I would never see. Of course, that is definitely a fantasy since I never buy lottery tickets.

You never know when the urge to dream will hit you. Often, it happens unconsciously. It could even be a form of procrastination. Images come and go often in a random order. It's a lovely escape from reality.

There's a similar but much more focused technique that many successful athletes, celebrities, and leaders use called visualization. Visualization is purposeful and planned. The idea is to see yourself doing the thing you want to accomplish. In your mind, you go through the steps necessary to achieve your goal.

> **Visualization is purposeful and planned. The idea is to see yourself doing the thing you want to accomplish. In your mind, you go through the steps necessary to achieve your goal.**

It turns out that your mind forms new neural pathways, whether you visualize it or actually do it. Athletes commonly use this technique. They play the game in their minds before they ever step onto the field. Each play or move they want to make has already occurred in their mind, so when they're actually playing, their mind and body know what to do.

Michael Phelps, the Olympic swimmer, practiced this technique regularly. He created the perfect tape of his race in his mind, and each night as he lay in bed, he visualized the race from start to finish. It helped him stay calm and confident before and during the actual race because he had swum it over and over again in his head. Visualization is a great tool that helped him win twenty-eight Olympic medals.

There's a famous story about Jim Carrey, the actor and comedian. Well before he was successful in 1985, he wrote himself a check for ten million dollars for "acting services rendered," dating it November 1995. He carried the check in his wallet and regularly visualized receiving the real thing. Just before Thanksgiving of 1995, he learned he was going to make ten million dollars for acting in the movie *Dumb and Dumber*.

Visualization isn't just about playing out a movie in your head. You need to engage all your senses. How will you feel? What will you hear? Is there a smell? Maybe you'll be tasting something.

It just doesn't work for athletes and celebrities. Regardless of your goals, it can work for you too. I've used it before when speaking to an audience. I see myself standing before the crowd, looking out, and impactfully delivering my message. Everyone is engaged and connecting with me. I hear the applause, and I imagine audience members coming up to me and sharing their positive feedback when I'm done.

I also use it when I have difficult conversations with people, both in a personal and professional setting. I imagine what I would say and how I think the other person would respond. I play out different scenarios, and when I sit down to actually have the discussion, I feel prepared.

Visualization isn't just about playing out a movie in your head. You need to engage all your senses. How will you feel? What will you hear? Is there a smell? Maybe you'll be tasting something.

As I was preparing to publish my memoir, I had the unimaginable goal of meeting Oprah and telling her how she impacted my life. I would share my journey that kickstarted in February 2020 when I heard her speech about secrets. It set me off on a trip with many twists and turns that eventually led to me writing my memoir, not to make money (although that would be nice), but to share my story with the world that'd inspire others to connect with their inner power and strength to change their lives as they see fit.

It had now been two-and-a-half years since that day, and I was holding my memoir, waiting for it to be released into the world. The next time Oprah was on stage, whether in person or on TV, I wanted to be there with her, sharing what I had learned, so I visualized Oprah and me chatting in front of a large audience. I wanted to be reminded of my dream, so I printed out a picture of Oprah interviewing Michelle Obama from that February day in Brooklyn. My goal was to have a picture of Oprah interviewing me, but I'm technologically challenged, so I printed out a picture of my face and pasted it over Michelle's (sorry about that, Michelle!).

I put it in a frame and placed it right beside my computer, so I could look at it every day and visualize our interview. One day, I opened my email to find a message from the Oprah Daily Insider that said Oprah would be taping a show about weight loss on July 31st in New York City. They were offering tickets to a small number of Oprah Daily Insider members. The email instructed us to only respond if we were sure we could attend along with a guest of our choice. I looked at my calendar and saw that the only day in a three-week period of time that I was free was on July 31st, so I replied.

The funny thing was that I had no idea why I got the email. I had forgotten I was an Insider member. I had become a member when I bought Oprah's journal months earlier, but I hadn't watched any of the videos or looked at resources inside the membership. I knew in my gut that I was meant to be in that audience. I visualized myself being there and handing my book to Oprah.

The morning of July 20th, I was doing some last-minute work before leaving for a family vacation. As I did every morning, I flipped my inspirational quotes calendar to the current date and read the quote: "You don't become what you want, you become what you believe." The quote was from Oprah Winfrey. Minutes later, I opened my email to find a personal email from a producer from *The Oprah Daily Show* asking me if I had ever struggled with my weight.

As I began to type my response, I started to tremble because I was scared to do what I was thinking of doing. Looking at the picture of me and Oprah along with her quote, I decided it was meant to be, so I continued typing: "I have so many stories about my own weight journey that I could write a book. LOL! I did write a book." I attached my manuscript to the email, pushing send before I could think about it any further, and left for vacation.

Each morning and afternoon while I was away, I checked my email, hoping to see a response, but there was nothing. July 31st was now only days away, and it looked like I wouldn't be in the audience. I decided that I needed to wipe the thought out of my mind and visualize a Harpo producer calling me to tell me I got the tickets.

For days, I laid on the beach with my eyes closed, visualizing that call coming in, but by the end of the vacation, there was radio silence. My sons and I were driving home on Friday, July 28th, when we stopped to grab a sandwich in a crowded Wawa at lunchtime. As I was deciding what I would eat, my phone rang. The name and number were unfamiliar, but I answered anyway. I had a feeling.

It was the Harpo producer. He had a few more questions for me, and it was obvious he never looked at or even noticed that I had attached my book to my response, but that was okay. He told me that he would let me know by the end of the day if I had secured a ticket. I'm not sure how I was even able to steer my car on the highway once we got back on the road. For the next few hours, I visualized the email that would let me know I was in. I visualized my cousin Mindy and me sitting in the audience with Oprah on a small stage.

When I arrived home, the email was waiting for me. Mindy and I were going to see Oprah. The email gave specific instructions and mentioned that there would be approximately one hundred people in the audience. With so few people in attendance, I figured I'd be able to give a copy of my book to one of the producers, who would then hopefully give it to Oprah. I wrote a message to Oprah inside the book, sharing that my goal was to inspire others just as she had inspired me. All weekend long, I created an image in my mind of Oprah holding my book. My hope was that she would be intrigued once she saw it, decide to read it, love it, and call me to tell me it was going to be part of her book club.

As we were escorted to our seats by one of the producers on July 31st, I thought about giving the book to the producer right there and then but decided to wait because a little piece of me hoped I might be able to hand it to Oprah herself. Even though I knew it was going to be a small audience, being there and seeing the intimate setting was exhilarating and gave me the chills.

We watched Oprah tape two different shows. In between the two, she went and changed her clothes, and the producers rearranged the audience. Initially, Mindy and I were in the fourth row, but for the second show, we were moved up to the second row in a different section of the audience. Oprah was friendly and chatty with the audience when the cameras weren't rolling. She had such a way of putting you at ease that you actually forgot you were there with Oprah.

Once the second show ended, Oprah chatted with audience members and even took selfies with them. I grabbed my book and went to the stage, waiting for her to come down the line to where I was standing. As I stood there clutching my book, I realized I had no idea what I was going to say to her. I hadn't mentally rehearsed this since I assumed I would only hand it to a producer.

My heart was pounding out of my chest when she approached me. She gave me her full attention as I told her how she changed my life in February 2020. She then asked me specifically what she had said that sparked my transformation, and I shared the story with her. As I held out the book to give to her, I explained how I had written about it in the book and how my goal was to inspire others just as she inspired me.

She took the book from me, read the title out loud, and thumbed through the pages. Our interaction ended there, and Oprah moved down the line to the next person with my memoir in her hands. As Mindy and I walked out, she stopped and asked what was wrong with me. I had no idea what she was talking about. She said, "You just spoke to Oprah and gave her your book, and you're so calm. I think you're in shock." She was right! "I just gave my book to Oprah," I squealed.

I reflected on the events that had taken place over the last couple of weeks, and there was something in my gut telling me this was going to happen. The act of visualizing what I wanted to happen had been so powerful that I wasn't surprised my vision became a reality. Of course, I didn't know if Oprah was going to read my book and decide to make it part of her book club, but that's a vision I'm still working on.

As I visualized each step, I saw it happen in my mind. I could feel the emotions. It felt real. It felt like it would happen. Up until that point, I hadn't made visualization a regular practice. I wanted to go to this event and give Oprah my book more than I had wanted anything, so I had pulled out all the stops.

Did it happen because I visualized it happening? I can't answer that with one-hundred percent confidence, but what I can tell you is that when I was visualizing, in my gut, I knew it would happen. I wasn't surprised that it did, and I felt prepared in the moment since I had been there already in my head.

So now, are you ready to put the book down, close your eyes, and visualize yourself chatting with Oprah? I'm certainly not guaranteeing that one, but what I can tell you is that I've found it to be an impactful tool. The problem for me is that it's one more thing that I *need* to do every day, and that feels overwhelming. If we put too much pressure on ourselves, we'll never wind up sticking with it. Sure, finding ten minutes each day to sit down and visualize our goals is ideal, but doing a little more than you do today is the way to get started. Start with once a week and then incrementally increase the amount of time.

If you've created more than one goal, choose one to begin with. Ideally, writing down the specific details of what you want to accomplish, including what you see, hear, smell, taste, and feel, is the place to start. It allows you to gain some clarity and really think it through. But if that doesn't work for you, don't let that stop you.

For me, the next step is planning when I'm going to visualize, because if I don't, it will never happen. It has to be one of those things that's on my calendar or that I incorporate into my morning or bedtime routine. At the same time, decide where you're going to do it. Make sure it's a place where you won't be distracted.

When you're ready to begin, take several deep breaths, close your eyes, and let your mind explore all the details. If you find yourself losing focus, that's okay and normal. Just bring yourself back, regardless of how often you drift. The more you practice, the better you'll get. This is a learned skill, so be kind to yourself. You're a novice.

Visualization isn't daydreaming; it's a real tool that can help bring your biggest dreams to life. Think of it like mapping out a route to where you want to go. The more clearly you can see your destination in your mind, the better your chances of getting there. Take a few minutes each day to picture your goals vividly. Imagine achieving them. How does it feel? What does it look like? Keep those images close and use them to fuel your journey. Let's make those dreams a reality, one vivid picture at a time!

> **Visualization isn't daydreaming; it's a real tool that can help bring your biggest dreams to life.**

Key Takeaways:

1. Picture Success: Visualization helps you see yourself achieving your goals, just like athletes do before a big game.

2. Use Your Senses: Make your mental movies vivid by imagining what you see, hear, and feel. The more detailed, the better!

3. Practice Regularly: Like any skill, the more you practice visualization, the better you get. Make it a habit to visualize your goals often for maximum impact.

Activities

Activity 1: Guided Visualization

Objective

Use guided imagery to enhance your ability to visualize with the help of a structured audio recording.

Materials Needed:

- Access to a guided visualization recording (many are available for free online or through apps)
- Headphones

Step 1: Find a Quiet Place

Ensure you are in a comfortable, quiet space where you won't be disturbed.

Step 2: Select a Guided Visualization

Choose a recording that best suits your goals. There are general visualizations or those targeted at specific outcomes (like achieving career goals, health, or personal happiness).

Step 3: Listen and Visualize

Put on your headphones, start the recording, and close your eyes. Follow the narrator's instructions, allowing your imagination to picture what's being described vividly.

Step 4: Visualization Practice

Regularly practicing guided visualization will train your brain to generate vivid mental images and emotions associated with your desired outcomes, enhancing your focus and motivation.

Activity 2: The "Perfect Day" Scenario

Objective

Develop your visualization skills by imagining your ideal perfect day from start to finish.

Materials Needed:

- Journal or a piece of paper
- Pen or pencil

Step 1: Find a Comfortable Spot

Sit in a quiet and comfortable place where you can think without interruptions.

Step 2: Imagine Your Perfect Day

Close your eyes and imagine your perfect day related to a specific goal you have. Picture everything from the moment you wake up. What do you see? What are you doing? Who are you with? How do you feel?

Step 3: Write It Down

Open your eyes and write down everything you visualized. Describe your surroundings, activities, people, conversations, and especially how you feel throughout the day.

Step 4: Practice Visualization

Revisit this exercise with varying focuses on different aspects of your life. Regular practice will improve your ability to visualize detailed scenarios, making your mental practice more effective in influencing your subconscious mind.

Activity 3: Vision Board Plus

Objective

Visually represent your dreams and add actionable steps.

Materials Needed:

- Magazines
- Poster Board
- Glue
- Scissors
- Markers
- Sticky Notes

Instructions:

1. Create a traditional vision board by cutting out images and words from magazines that align with your dreams and gluing them to the poster board.

2. Use sticky notes to write down one action you can take for each image or word to bring you closer to that vision. Stick these notes around the border of your vision board.

3. Place your vision board somewhere you will see it every day and make a weekly plan to tackle one of the actions noted on your sticky notes.

Journal Prompt

Write a letter to yourself five years in the future, imagining that you've achieved all your current dreams. Describe your life, how you feel, and the journey you took to get there.

Seal the letter in an envelope and set a date in the future to open it. You might also choose to share this letter with a trusted friend or family member who can send it back to you at the right time.

9

A Sprinkle of Action

MAGENTA:
Intense and impactful, magenta represents decisive and dynamic action.

You're ready! All the work we've done together up until now has been critical to setting the proper foundation; however, none of it means much if we don't take action. Without action, everything that came before are just dreams and plans.

Yet, many people never take the first step and start. Many are afraid they aren't ready. They haven't

> **Without action, everything that came before are just dreams and plans.**

done enough planning or research yet. They think it isn't the perfect time to start. Is it ever? No. It's never the perfect time, and there will always be more you could do to prepare, so why are you allowing that to stop you? The answer is, most likely, fear.

Many of us share the same fear: the fear of failure. Failing often makes us feel ashamed or embarrassed. Of course, if I try something and no one else knows, then it will er. I am a former smoker. I started smoking when I was thirteen years old, which sounds absurd to say out loud now. Back then, both my parents smoked, and the general public was just becoming aware of how bad it was. We could smoke anywhere and everywhere—restaurants, malls, airplanes, movie theaters, etc. Once I was in my twenties, some of those privileges were removed, and the public perception of smokers was shifting. I loved smoking, and the idea of quitting was unbearable. I was becoming self-conscious about being a smoker, but not enough to do anything about it.

When I was twenty-seven years old, I came down with a bad case of mononucleosis and had to take disability leave from my job for six weeks. One morning, after dragging myself out of bed to go to the bathroom, I lit up a cigarette and almost hacked up a lung. I realized how insane it was to smoke when feeling so sick. I decided I could do without another cigarette until the afternoon. Just so you understand, I smoked a pack and a half a day, so going without a cigarette for hours was something I did not do.

As the clock struck two, I realized I hadn't smoked and wasn't feeling the need to have a cigarette, so I increased my target to the evening. Feeling no better, I fell asleep that night only having smoked one cigarette that day, the one I had first thing in the morning. I continued this little game the next day and the next but never told anyone. I hit the three-day mark without a cigarette and toyed with the idea of quitting.

What if I told everyone I was quitting, but once I felt better, I started smoking again? I'd look like a failure, and it would only prove that I have no discipline, just like with dieting. I couldn't risk the humiliation, so I didn't let anyone know that I hadn't smoked in days. I had many arguments with myself over the idea of quitting. Deep down, I knew that if I didn't quit now, I would need to quit in the future. At least I had a head start and hadn't suffered in the beginning as most reformed smokers do since I was already feeling so lousy.

I knew that once I said to another person out loud that I was quitting, everything would change. On the one hand, being held accountable could help when refraining became difficult, but *what if I broke down and smoked? Then what would people think of me?* At once, all my limiting beliefs flooded my brain. *You're not good enough. You're too lazy. You have no discipline.* After days of deliberation, despite those thoughts, on day six, I said it out loud. I am quitting.

And since that day, some thirty-five years ago, I have never touched a cigarette again.

The goal of quitting smoking felt impossible to achieve, but when I took small, micro-actions, it was easier. I didn't start by quitting; instead, I played a game with myself, and when I had success, like not smoking for a few hours, it propelled me to keep going. Achievement felt good, and I wanted more of it.

Today, one of the practices that helps me is taking time each morning to fill out my journal by listing the three actions I will take that day to move me closer to my main goal. I also write a to-do list of the things that aren't as important but need to get done. Now, the hard part is taking that journal with me to the office and keeping it open on my desk, reminding myself of my daily goals.

When I first started this habit, I considered myself successful if I brought my planner with me and then actually took it out of my bag, opened it up, and looked at it during the day. Even if I didn't take the three small actions I had written down, I had accomplished something. Most of the time, when I did look at the journal several times in a day, I would complete the daily tasks. I was in charge of my day. Even when unforeseen circumstances came up, which they always do, I had a clear picture in my mind of what I wanted to accomplish.

In my life prior to the age of fifty, I let the events of the day lead the way. The circumstances of my life were in charge, not me. Now, it's marvelously rewarding to know that each day I have a goal, direction, and purpose. Talk about empowering! Once you get a taste of it, you'll want more.

Getting in the habit of doing the hard stuff first is another great tool. I don't know about you, but I'd much rather start my day by doing the easy tasks first so I can cross a lot of things off my list while putting off the activities I find challenging. You know that feeling when you look at the clock, it's 3 p.m., and you haven't accomplished what you set out to do? At that point, you tell yourself that you don't have time and promise yourself that you'll do it tomorrow.

Tomorrow is a repeat of today. And you wonder why you're not making progress. If you find yourself in this loop, it could mean that your planned daily activities need to be broken down further into smaller steps. I feel your eyes roll when I say that. Those tiny steps feel like a waste of time, and they are not getting you anywhere. However, think about if, every day for a year, you inched little by little towards your goal. Let's say that you spend fifteen minutes, five days a week, working towards your goal. That would translate into sixty-five hours. Chances are, if you weren't intentional, that total would be zero.

Taking action is not easy, but it's necessary. Do you enjoy paying your bills? Cleaning the house? Being stuck in traffic? What would happen if you didn't do these things? You would most likely be out on the streets without a way to earn a living. We all do these non-preferred activities because we feel we have to, when really we do have a choice. We are choosing between living with a roof over our head or not. In order to get our desired outcome, we take action.

As we reflect back on our lives, it is all a result of the choices we make and the actions we take. In *Atomic Habits*, James Clear explains, "Every action you take is a vote for the type of person you wish to become." Taking action is what stands between us and our goals, but it often feels overwhelming. If I had known what I was getting myself into when I first decided to write a book, I'm not sure if I would have taken action. Instead, the actions needed were presented one by one, making it more digestible. Even if we do know all the steps necessary, we must only focus on the one right in front of us.

Taking action is what stands between us and our goals, but it often feels overwhelming.

We want to start with a sprinkle of action or one very small step that feels doable. If your goal was to run a marathon and you never ran at all, would you go out and run twenty-six miles? You could try, but chances are good that you won't make it, become discouraged, and quit. Instead, if you decide to start with a small action and take a walk around the block, you'll be on your way.

Recently, an acquaintance complimented me on all I've accomplished over the past few years. She went on to share how she discovered a project she started three years ago but never finished. She found it collecting dust in a pile. Can you relate? I certainly can. She shared with me that she wondered where she would be now if she had completed that project three years ago. She'll never know. Is that what you want for yourself?

Taking action might seem daunting at first, but remember, it's the most essential step in turning your dreams into reality. You've prepared, you've planned, and you've dreamed—now it's time to act. Don't wait for the perfect moment; it might never come. Start small, keep it simple, and push through the fear. Each little step you take is a big leap towards your goals. Let's get moving and make things happen. Your future is waiting for you to shape it, one action at a time.

Taking action might seem daunting at first, but remember, it's the most essential step in turning your dreams into reality.

Key Takeaways:

1. Start Small: Tackle your goals with small, manageable steps. This makes the process less daunting and helps you get going without feeling overwhelmed.

2. Face Your Fears: Don't let the fear of messing up hold you back. Remember, taking action is always better than doing nothing. Every step forward is progress.

3. Stay Consistent: Keep at it, even if the steps are tiny. Regular effort adds up, turning small actions into big achievements over time. It's all about keeping the momentum going!

tinue asking why until you get to the real reason. Here's an example:

Why have you decided to start a business?
So I can make more money.
Why do you want to make more money?
So I never need to worry about paying my bills, and I can spend money on whatever I want without thinking about it.
Why do you need to stop worrying?
So I can be relaxed and spend more time with my family.
Why do you want to be relaxed and spend more time with your family?
Because in the past, there have been times when I've missed out on enjoying them because I was stressed and uptight. I was never really present because I had too much on my mind.
Why do you need to be present?
My family is everything to me. Creating memories together, loving each other, and being there for one another is all I want.
This is the real "why."

The next time I struggle to do the hard thing, I remind myself why I'm doing it in the first place. You could write that "why" on an index card and tape it to your computer or set reminders on your phone. Schedule daily reminders several times a day so you're continually reminding yourself of your "why."

Once you have your "why" in place, you're ready to move on to the next step. I discovered that having a morning routine was crucial to ensuring a productive day. My old morning routine was getting up with just enough time to

10

A Sprinkle of Discipline

GRAY:
Steady and unwavering, gray reflects the stability and structure of discipline.

Now you're on a roll. You're doing it. Change has begun, and it's exhilarating until, BOOM, you hit that wall. All of a sudden, it feels hard. You start to question yourself. *Is this really worth all this effort? There are so many other things I could be doing instead. This will never work anyway.*

Sound familiar? I'm guessing it does. Change is not easy; it's hard. It is so much easier to stay in your comfort zone, but where's that going to get you? You need to persevere. Each of us needs to figure out how. The same methods won't work for everyone, so let me offer a sprinkle of ideas.

The first is to figure out your "why." Why have you decided to embark on this journey of transformation in the first place? Write down the answer to this question and con-

> **The first is to figure out your "why." Why have you decided to embark on this journey of transformation in the first place?**

Activity 3: The Five Minute Challenge

Objective
Overcome procrastination and kickstart action by tackling tasks that can be completed in just five minutes.

Instructions:

1. Make a list of small tasks related to your goals that can be completed in five minutes or less.

2. Each day, randomly select one task from your list and commit to completing it within five minutes.

3. Use a timer to keep yourself on track. The pressure of the timer can help you focus your efforts and make the task feel like a fun challenge.

4. After completing the task, note how it felt to accomplish something quickly and how it contributed to your larger goals.

5. Gradually increase the complexity or duration of tasks as you build confidence and momentum for taking action.

Journal Prompt

Reflect on a time when inaction held you back from reaching a goal. What fears or beliefs contributed to your inaction? How did you, or could you, overcome these barriers to take action?

Activities

Activity 1: The Micro-Action Plan

Objective

Initiate progress towards a goal through micro-actions.

Instructions:

1. Choose a goal or project you've been putting off.

2. Break down the goal into the smallest possible actions, actions so small that they seem almost too easy to accomplish.

3. Commit to completing one micro-action per day. Track your progress and celebrate each step, no matter how small.

Activity 2: Daily Intentions Journal

Objective

Set daily intentions that support your larger goals and reflect on your progress to continuously improve your effectiveness and productivity.

Start each day by writing down one to three small intentions that align with your larger goals. These should be specific, achievable actions you can complete within the day.

Review these intentions at the end of the day to reflect on your progress. If you were unable to accomplish them, analyze why, so you can adjust the following day.

brush my teeth, shower, dress, and eat breakfast. I'd then grab my things and race off to work, hoping there was no traffic; otherwise, I would be late. I was stressed when I arrived because I had been racing against the clock all morning. I'd been living this way my whole life and hadn't realized there might be a better way to start my day.

Being forced to complete a morning journal in the first course I took changed my mind, seeing the trouble with my lifelong habit. Taking the time each morning to actually breathe without rushing was an eye-opener. My shoulders could relax, and my heart was no longer pounding. *I could get used to this.* Sitting down and gathering my thoughts and intentions for the day was empowering. I was the one in control of how my day was going to go. I was not gambling and leaving it up to chance.

I bought different journals to see which I liked the best, and I found I actually liked a combination, so I created my own by changing some of the prompts the author had on the page to ones I preferred. Here are the prompts I used with my answers from April 26, 2021:

Main goal I'm working on: I will reach my Weight Watchers goal and lose one hundred pounds. (I consciously decided not to add a timeframe. It's impossible to predict how quickly your body will decide to let go of those extra pounds).

Three actions you will take today to move you in the direction of your goal:

1. Eat 28-30 points (a Weight Watchers thing at the time.)

2. Attend 6 p.m. Zumba class.
3. Go food shopping.

Daily Affirmations:

I am creating the life of my dreams.
I accomplish everything I set my mind to.
I am welcoming all the ways the universe wants to bless me.
I am passionate about my goals and have a burning desire to fulfill them.
Today is going to be the best day ever!

Three other actions to help move me closer to other goals:

1. Work on plans to celebrate Mom's birthday.
2. Clean up and organize papers on my desk.
3. Talk to Gary about iron infusion. (Be compassionate, kind, and patient.)

To Do List:

1. Make doctors' appointment for Gary.
2. Transfer money from credit union to bank.
3. Bring laundry upstairs.
4. Go to Costco.
5. Make dinner reservations for Thursday.

Many days, my actions were the same, and some of the things on the to-do list would stay there for days. As soon as I finished, I would put the journal on top of my purse so I would remember to bring it with me to the office. Once there, I would open it up and read what I had written to remind myself of my plan. Referring back to it and checking actions off my list as I completed them brought a smile to my face. I was doing it. Day by day, step by step, I was taking consistent action towards my goals. My body tingled with pride and excitement.

Now, when I hit roadblocks, it was time to take a look at the daily actions I planned. *Were they too time-consuming? Is it too difficult? What's stopping me? Can I break this action down into a few simple steps?*

Using the example above, instead of my action of eating twenty-eight to thirty points, I could break it down to eating seven points for breakfast. Maybe that is the only goal I have for days or weeks until I have it down. I could then set a lunch goal and repeat. It's more manageable and realistic if I am having difficulty consistently eating that many points a day.

The next step is to find an accountability partner to help keep you on track. When it came to my Weight Watcher points, I knew each week I was checking in with someone who would weigh me and ask about my week. It's so much easier to quit when you're the only person you are answering to. In addition, your accountability partner will offer support and advice. They are there to be your biggest cheerleader and motivator. If you're truly serious about your goal, why wouldn't you want an accountability partner?

Writing my memoir, *On Second Thought... Maybe I Can!* most likely would never have happened without my accountability group. I never had a desire to write a book. There was nothing about it that I found appealing. I was the person in college who tried to only take classes that didn't require term papers (do they even call it that anymore?). If it was a required course and I had no choice, I was the biggest procrastinator when it came time to write. Instead of sitting down to actually work on it, I would spend the time complaining about it and dreading it.

So how the heck am I now writing my second book? Good question!

You see, once I discovered that each of us has the power to change our lives, I wanted to stand on my roof with a megaphone, letting everyone know. In all honesty, I've never been on my roof and am not really keen on the idea, and even with the megaphone, I would not reach enough people. So I needed a different plan. I landed on the idea of writing a book. The only problem with this idea is that I didn't know how to write one.

One day, I was listening to a podcast that I didn't listen to on a regular basis. The host was interviewing a woman who helped first-time authors get their stories out into the world. As I listened, I was drawn to this woman and felt that if I was ever really going to write a book, I would need help, and this woman seemed to be speaking my language. So, I booked an appointment to meet with her, and we connected instantly.

She was getting ready to launch a twelve-week course for first-time authors, and I got off the call feeling motivated to join but still a bit unsure. As I spent the next few days mulling it over, my husband and I received the very unexpected news that he had a form of blood cancer called myelodysplastic syndrome, and in his case, there was no cure. The doctor wouldn't give us any type of timeframe but only shared that he had an aggressive type of the disease.

Needless to say, my world was turned upside down in an instant.

I researched and researched and researched, and on my own, I determined that he'd be lucky to live for a year. For a week or so, I forgot all about the course and the book until one day I found myself telling my therapist about it. I was embarrassed to even bring it up to her when my husband was dying. *She's going to think I'm so selfish or self-absorbed. She's going to think I don't care about my husband.* When I introduced the topic, I started by saying, "I know this is ridiculous, and of course this is not the time, but…"

Her answer shocked me. She felt this was the perfect time for me to take this course and start writing. She said it would give me something else to focus on while living through a very challenging time. I signed up for the course, which included a weekly group call. Our group formed an immediate bond, and I looked forward to seeing everyone each Friday. At the end of our session, we shared our goals for the coming week, which we would review together the following week. I certainly didn't want to be the only one not achieving my goal, so I set out to figure out a way to make sure that I wrote something on most days, despite the daily challenges my family was facing.

When Gary was in the hospital, I would bring my computer, food, and drinks with me each day and set up shop in his hospital room. When he was sleeping, I would write. Once he was home and we settled into some sort of routine that revolved around doctors, medication, online therapy sessions, and chemotherapy (to try and slow the progression of the disease), I would schedule an hour of writing time into my calendar. Sometimes, it would be at six in the morning before Gary woke up, and other times I would jump on a co-writing session with my group.

At first, I really didn't even understand the idea of a co-writing session because you basically say hello to each other, someone sets a timer, and then you turn off your camera and sound and just write. When the timer goes off, you turn everything back on to say goodbye. It seemed silly, but I was wrong. If I signed up to attend and didn't show up, people would ask me where I was. It was yet another way I was being held accountable. Of course, there were some days when things didn't go as planned for one reason or another, and I would make sure to figure out what I needed to do the next day in order to get that writing time in.

As the course progressed, Gary's condition worsened, and he had several complications. I could have let that deter me, but I didn't. It was up to me to make it happen. I could have easily set it aside. I can't imagine there would be anyone who wouldn't have understood my decision to do that, but I was committed to my goal.

Gary died suddenly on December 30, 2022. I was three chapters shy of finishing my first draft. My draft was due to the editor on January 14, 2023, and naturally, my publisher offered to extend the deadline under the circumstances, but I declined. I hadn't come this far to not finish what I set out to accomplish.

I met the deadline and found myself beaming with pride as I pressed send, messaging my accountability group to share the news with them. If I had been doing this on my own, I guarantee the book would never have been written. Signing up for the course gave me accountability. It was the same with Weight Watchers. But what if you can't find an accountability partner already in place? You need to create one.

Regardless of whether you want a group or one individual, it's up to you to go out and find them. It could be a friend, acquaintance, or colleague. Maybe it's someone online that you met in a group. Approach them and explain your goal and what you're looking for. How would you like to communicate with them? Email? Text? Phone call? How often would you like to check in? Will you also be their accountability partner to help them achieve their goal? Together, you create the rules.

One last strategy that I'll share with you is to make this fun! I love to make it into a game by offering myself rewards as I reach small milestones. For me, it helps if I have a visual representation of my game, like a chart similar to a chore chart your child might have. You're the creator, so you determine what the rewards are if you win, as well as what constitutes success. Make sure not to make it too difficult; otherwise, it might be discouraging.

When I was writing my memoir, I had a goal to write a minimum of fifteen minutes a day, five days a week. Often, I exceeded the fifteen-minute goal, but at least fifteen minutes didn't feel so difficult. I had a weekly chart and would give myself a gold star each time I wrote for fifteen minutes. If I accomplished my goal for the week, I would get a prize. The prize could be going out to dinner or buying myself a small trinket. Seeing the gold stars from previous days helped me stay motivated. *Who doesn't want more gold stars?*

There are countless other strategies out there to help you develop discipline. The important thing to remember is that we all struggle with discipline, even those who make it look like they don't. It's all about experimenting and figuring out what is helpful for you. I'm always listening and learning about what other people do because the more ideas we have in our pocket to tap into when the going gets tough, the better.

Each small action you take is building your future, piece by piece. Remember, discipline isn't just about toughing it out; it's about setting yourself up for the kind of life you really want.

Remember, discipline isn't just about toughing it out; it's about setting yourself up for the kind of life you really want.

You've got this. As the renowned motivational speaker and author George Zalucki said, "Commitment is doing the thing you said you would do, long after the mood you said it in has left you."

Keep pushing forward, stay true to your plan, and watch as every little effort adds up. Every day you stick with it, you're not just dreaming—you're doing. Let's keep that momentum going and turn your dreams into reality. You're more ready than you think!

"Commitment is doing the thing you said you would do, long after the mood you said it in has left you."

George Zalucki

Key Takeaways:

1. Find Your Why: Understanding your deeper motivation helps sustain discipline. Knowing why you're pursuing a goal provides clarity and fuels your perseverance, especially when challenges arise.

2. Set Up Routines: A consistent routine can be a game-changer. It puts you in control and sets the tone for a productive day, helping you stick to your plan and move closer to your goals.

3. Seek Support: Don't do it alone! Finding someone to share your journey with can make a huge difference. An accountability partner not only motivates you but also celebrates your successes and supports you through challenges.

Activities

Activity 1: The Accountability Pact

Objective

Build accountability for taking consistent action towards your goals.

Instructions:

1. Identify a friend, family member, or coworker who also has a goal they're working towards.

2. Make a pact to hold each other accountable for taking daily or weekly steps towards your respective goals.

3. Schedule a regular check-in to update each other on your progress, challenges, and successes.

Activity 2: The Distraction List

Objective

Identify and mitigate distractions that hinder your ability to maintain discipline.

Instructions:

1. Over the course of one week, keep a log of moments when you find yourself distracted from your tasks.

2. Categorize these distractions (e.g., social media, unnecessary interruptions, multitasking).

e end of the week, review your list and deter-
 which distractions are the most frequent.

lop a strategy to reduce or eliminate these top distractions from your work environment.

Activity 3: The 21-Day Discipline Challenge

Objective

Establish and reinforce a new habit that contributes to your larger goal.

Instructions:

1. Choose one small action you can take every day that will build discipline and contribute to your goal (e.g., waking up at a certain time, exercising for thirty minutes, reading industry-related material for fifteen minutes).

2. Commit to doing this action every day for twenty-one days, tracking your progress on a calendar or journal.

3. Reflect daily on how this activity is helping to build your discipline and how it's impacting your progress towards your goals.

Journal Prompt

Reflect on a past experience where maintaining discipline led to a positive outcome. What strategies did you use to stay focused, and how can you apply them to current challenges?

11

A Sprinkle of Adaptability

TEAL:
Fluid and versatile, teal mirrors the flexibility and adaptiveness required in change.

Life never goes as planned. Just when you think you have everything figured out, something unexpected pops up and throws you off course. It might be a change at work, a personal challenge, or something else entirely. These moments test our ability to adapt and keep moving forward. Adaptability isn't simply about dealing with these bumps in the road; it's about thriving despite them. It's the skill that turns setbacks into opportunities for growth.

Think about a time when, all of a sudden, your efforts no longer made sense or you didn't see a way forward. The old you would have thrown your hands up in the air and quit, blaming the person or event that caused you to fail. However, that's not the "you" that's going to show up now. Nope! I just won't allow it.

Did Thomas Edison give up when his attempts at creating the light bulb failed? No, he did not. He treated each failure as a step towards his success. He famously said, "I have not failed. I've just found ten thousand ways that won't work." He viewed his so-called failures as a lesson. Edison gained knowledge with each attempt, and the same holds true for you.

Sometimes, we are so locked into our goals and vision that it's very easy to be derailed when we see it in black and white. Either we succeed or not. Unfortunately or fortunately—however you see it—it doesn't work that way. We need to be flexible and adaptable. If we hit a roadblock, we need to either figure out a way around it or make a sharp right turn. It can be very discouraging and feel like you've wasted time, effort, and money. When you find yourself in that situation, I want you to look at a lamp and think of Edison.

Back in 2021, I formed the Caregiver Support Squad, which had a mission to help family caregivers learn to prioritize their self-care. I was excited and went all in. I hired a business coach and paid several thousand dollars to build a website. I was on my way—taking action every day, some days less than others, but still making progress.

The day finally arrived when I began to coach someone and get my business started. I was meeting with a fellow caregiver online to help them learn how to take care of themselves. I wasn't charging for my time as this was part of a certified caregiver consultant certification I was pursuing. I prepared feverishly for our hour-long appointment, making sure I had all my resources handy. I dedicated the first ten minutes to hearing their caregiving story. As my client shared, I listened intently and asked her questions, trying to understand the situation.

Adaptability isn't simply about dealing with these bumps in the road; it's about thriving despite them. It's the skill that turns setbacks into opportunities for growth.

Anytime I tried to steer the conversation towards her own care, she launched into a long explanation of why it wasn't possible. I kept hearing about her loved ones' health problems, which led to money problems (which is often the case when a loved one is ill or disabled for an extended period of time). By the end of the conversation, which actually lasted eighty-five minutes, not sixty, I ended the meeting feeling defeated.

All the things I thought we'd discuss and the tools I would share never happened. It's possible the client found it helpful because it always feels good to share your story and get things off your chest. However, there wasn't much discussion about self-care. At that particular time in my life, I was in the midst of my own caregiving journey for my husband, who was suffering from a variety of unrelated physical and mental illnesses prior to receiving the cancer diagnosis.

Gary's depression was seeping into all aspects of my life, and even when I attempted to compartmentalize my feelings, this discussion with another caregiver triggered my emotions. Prior to our appointment, I was hopeful and energized, but by the end, I found myself feeling down. I told myself this could be an isolated incident and that I needed to try again.

I organized a virtual small group get-together with a few caregivers, hoping this would lead to a better outcome. We all shared our stories and sympathized with one another, which was a lovely bonding experience, but when I introduced the topic of self-care, the excuses started to fly. When pushed, a couple of women gave a specific example of what self-care activities they would try to incorporate into their lives, but it seemed to me an insincere attempt to pacify me. I could have been wrong, but when I followed up via email, the response rate was low.

All of the air drained out of me like a balloon. *I was a failure.* I invested all this time and money into creating the Caregiver Support Squad, and it was a bust. I needed a few days to digest everything. As I saw it, I had two choices: I could continue on this path, figuring out how to tweak what I was doing to see if it would lead to a better outcome, or I could put the Caregiver Support Squad to rest.

I chose option number two.

I knew I hadn't even come close to giving it a fair chance, but I realized I didn't have the emotional capacity at this point in my life to take on other people's caregiving issues. I'm an empathetic person, so as I listen, I'm always trying to figure out a solution to their problems. I leave these conversations carrying the weight of their struggles as well as mine, and I was operating at maximum capacity. For my own mental well-being, I had no choice.

So, now what? If I'm not going to help caregivers, what else can I do? Who else am I qualified to help? Shana, my coach, took me through a series of exercises, helping me dig deep to figure out what I really wanted. Simultaneously, I worked with Alex Street, who is a story coach. I know, it sounds crazy, right? A story coach—what the heck is that? Well, you share your life story, and he helps you make sense of it in a way that you can own what you've learned and use it to help others.

Working with Alex brought so much clarity. He described my life story in a way I had never thought of before. He explained how I lived my life being told I couldn't do something, either from others or myself. I lived my life that way until I turned fifty, had the AHA moment, and then changed my mindset to "maybe I can." I was floored. I had never analyzed my life from that perspective. He was right. I hadn't given myself any credit for the fact that I had slowly changed my life since turning fifty.

Isn't it funny how so often it takes someone else to point out something that really should have been obvious to you?

Alex helped me see how my personal life journey thus far had been piecemealed together. It was a guessing game; some games I won and others I did not. I could be a one-stop shop to guide women on their own journey to a life they construct for themselves. Did you see me do that whoopie jump in my bedroom? Because that's what I was doing when no one was watching.

I was ready to figure out how to move forward in a new direction and leave the Caregiver Support Squad behind.

You and I are adapting all the time. Think about what you do on a daily basis. You are taking in feedback, looking for clues to see if you need to change something. Parenting is a great example. You handle something one way, let's say by giving your daughter a time out, but she continues to engage in unacceptable behavior. If you see it's not working, you would most likely try another approach; maybe give positive reinforcement a go. You would continue to monitor, analyze, and adjust.

> **You and I are adapting all the time.**

In your professional life, you are attuned to changes in the market or your customer preferences. It might be a signal that you need to pivot. You might also notice that the direction you're headed doesn't feel right, or it's causing undue stress, just as the Caregiver Support Squad was doing to me.

Recognizing the signals that it might be time to make a change is the first step. In order to move forward, you need to take a step back and objectively analyze the situation. Chances are you already have your own method of assessing a situation; if so, that's great. Even if you do, it's always worth exploring something different to see if it changes your perspective. Here are a few ideas:

1. SWOT Analysis: SWOT stands for strengths, weaknesses, opportunities, and threats. The idea is to make four separate lists for the above-mentioned categories. Doing so helps you analyze the current situation. This method is often used in business but could certainly be applied on a personal level as well.

2. Pros and Cons List: The old-fashioned make a list of all the pros and cons. It works, and I personally find this very helpful in all areas of life. Taking the time to create the list and seeing it on paper (or a computer screen) allows you to clearly see the situation.

3. Consultation: Discuss with a counselor, friend, or associate. Talking it out brings clarity, not to mention you get someone else's opinion. Please be sure you are discussing this with someone whose opinion you value.

4. Go With Your Gut: Tap into your intuition and listen to what your gut is telling you. This method is not

analytical or scientifically based, but I believe your gut doesn't lie.

Once you've decided on your new direction, repeat the process of establishing your vision, taking action, and remaining disciplined. Of course, on paper, it sounds so simple, but it's not. The more you embrace flexibility, the easier it becomes. I recently heard someone define failure as **F**irst **A**ttempt **I**n **L**earning. Remember, it's all about embracing that growth mindset we discussed early on in Chapter Two. Learning, embracing challenges, and being flexible keep us moving forward in this exciting game of life.

Life is full of surprises and changes, and how we adjust to them makes all the difference. Don't get discouraged by setbacks; instead, use them as opportunities to grow and learn. Stay open to change, ready to shift gears when needed. Adapting isn't just about surviving; it's about thriving. Keep moving forward, keep adjusting, and keep your goals in sight. You've got this!

> **Don't get discouraged by setbacks; instead, use them as opportunities to grow and learn.**

Key Takeaways:

1. Embrace Flexibility: Life's unexpected challenges are opportunities to learn and grow. Being flexible allows you to navigate these challenges effectively, continually progressing towards your goals.

2. Reframe Setbacks as Lessons: Like Thomas Edison's approach to inventing the light bulb, view each setback as a step closer to success, not as a failure. This mindset transforms obstacles into steppingstones.

3. Adaptability Is Essential for Growth: Constantly evaluate and adjust your strategies in response to life's changes. This adaptability not only helps in overcoming obstacles but also in seizing new opportunities that arise.

Activities

Activity 1: Embrace the Obstacle

Objective

Transform obstacles into opportunities for growth.

Instructions:

1. Identify a significant obstacle you're currently facing.

2. Consider how this obstacle can be viewed as an opportunity for learning or direction change. Ask yourself what new skills, insights, or connections you can gain from addressing this challenge.

3. Write a plan that includes at least one actionable step you can take to leverage this obstacle as a growth opportunity.

Activity 2: The Adaptability Journal

Objective

Cultivate a mindset that embraces change and adaptability.

Instructions:

1. Keep a daily or weekly journal to write about and reflect on moments where you had to adapt to unexpected circumstances.

2. For each entry, jot down the situation, how you adapted (or struggled to adapt), and what you learned from the experience.

3. Regularly review your journal entries to identify patterns in how you deal with change and areas where you can improve your adaptability.

Activity 3: Feedback Loops

Objective:

Actively seek and integrate feedback for continuous adaptation.

Steps:

1. Choose an area of your life or a specific project where feedback could be beneficial.

2. Identify at least three people whose opinions you value and ask them for specific feedback on this area or project.

3. Analyze the feedback for common themes and identify one action you can take to adjust based on this feedback.

Journal Prompt

Write about a time when being flexible or changing your plan led to an unexpected success. How did adaptability play a role in this outcome?

12

A Sprinkle of Resilience

INDIGO:
Deep and resilient, indigo reflects the inner strength and endurance of resilience.

"Resilience is more than just bouncing back from adversity. It's our ability to move through difficult times, learn from them, and continue to grow and thrive. It involves developing a mindset that allows us to see challenges as opportunities for growth." — Brené Brown, PhD, LMSW, research professor at the University of Houston and bestselling author.

Have you ever lost a job? Lost a loved one? Had relationship issues? Health problems? Became a caregiver? If you answered no to all these questions, it's highly likely that, at some point in your life, the answer will be yes because struggles are a part of life. Many of these are out of our control, but remember that how we respond is one-hundred percent in our control.

Nelson Mandela is an excellent example of resilience. He was imprisoned for over twenty-seven years for his efforts to end racial segregation in South Africa. Once

"Resilience is more than just bouncing back from adversity. It's our ability to move through difficult times, learn from them, and continue to grow and thrive."

Brené Brown

released, he didn't give up the fight. The harshness of his imprisonment fueled his fire instead of stopping it. In the end, his resilience and perseverance led to his election as the first black president of South Africa.

"Oh, you're so strong!"

"I could never do what you do."

"I don't know how you do it."

People have said these things to me since I was in my twenties. In the beginning, my chest would swell with pride, but over time, I grew to resent those comments. *What choice did I have? If I didn't keep going, what would happen to everyone else? You don't know how you would react until you're in the situation, and lucky for you, you're not.*

I didn't ask to have so many challenges in my life. Who would? For most of my life, it was as if I kept a tally, convinced I had the most marks on the list. *But why me?* This question used to drive me crazy. I would wrack my brain trying to figure out what I had done to deserve a life filled with so many burdens.

The funny thing is that all those obstacles actually helped build my resilience. Little did I know that they were preparing me for my greatest challenge—becoming a widow.

As I mentioned earlier, my husband, Gary, was ill for several years. In the last ten years of his life, I watched him decline both physically and mentally. He didn't take care of himself, regardless of the countless doctor appointments I made for him. Whether he would show up for them depended on what his mental state was that particular day. He was battling serious depression and anxiety, and he wasn't properly treated for it. He was on medication, but with mental illness, there is not one pill that works for everyone. It's trial and error, and even if it seems to work for a while, it can suddenly become ineffective.

For years, I was angry with him because he wouldn't attend family gatherings. Our kids were preteens, and I hated that he was often not present. We wouldn't know if he was going to come with us until the day arrived. I'd spend weeks prior trying to figure out what I could do or say to him to make him see the importance of his attendance. As I learned over the years, logic often doesn't work when you're dealing with someone who suffers from depression and anxiety.

Going out to dinner, something we enjoyed doing as a couple and as a family, became impossible for him. I attended every social gathering alone, often feeling uncomfortable and upset. I wanted my husband there with me. I wanted the Gary I knew and loved to show up—the man everyone loved because he was warm, funny, and engaging. *Where did he go?*

The years passed and his conditions worsened, but I always held out hope. *Maybe this new psychiatrist, therapist, or doctor could make him better.* We were shocked when we found out that in addition to all his physical illnesses, and there were many, he had myelodysplastic syndrome (MDS), a form of blood cancer.

Even though I had effectively lost my marriage and partner years earlier, he was still physically with me. This diagnosis stripped away any glimmer of hope that I held. Now, it was just a matter of time. The last six months of his life were brutal. He was in and out of hospitals with different infections, and with each hospitalization, his depression worsened. It finally led to his being involuntarily committed to a mental hospital.

    I was gutted. Watching him suffer, watching my kids suffer, and constantly thinking about the inevitable. On the one hand, I longed for his suffering to end, but on the other hand, I didn't want him to die. I spent hours Googling, trying to figure out how long he had to live. I created different scenarios in my mind of how it would happen.

    When it did happen, I wasn't prepared, even after all the visualization I had done. He hadn't been feeling well but refused to go to the doctor. The prior week when we were there, his blood levels were actually decent, so I didn't think there was anything imminent. It turns out he had pneumonia, and by the time he agreed to have me call an ambulance, he was really struggling to breathe.

    He went into respiratory failure in the ambulance, where they intubated him. Less than a day later, I stood next to him with my hand on his shoulder as they began to stop his IV's, and it was over. All of my so-called preparation made no difference. The fact that he had stopped being my partner years before no longer mattered. The only thing that mattered was that I loved him, despite all our struggles, and I wasn't prepared to live the rest of my life without him.

    We were together for thirty years—half of my life. My boys lost their father. It wasn't supposed to be this way. Even though Gary wasn't able to help much with household management or parenting, he was still there. I could run some things by him if he was in a decent mood. He knew me better than anyone else on the planet. We had been through so much together. I never felt more alone. The loneliness caused me to physically hurt. It was almost comical that I thought I was prepared.

After the first week or two, when my loved ones went back to their own lives, reality kicked in. Every minute of every day felt different. Gary had been sleeping downstairs in a room I turned into a bedroom for him, but even though I slept alone for over a year, lying in bed by myself was tough. Knowing he wasn't in the house turned me into a light sleeper. My boys were both there for the first month, but it still felt quiet and empty.

Grieving is an individual process. Each of us goes through it in our own way and in our own time. There is no right or wrong. Sure, I had days and nights when I couldn't function, but I knew I needed to still live. I had people who still depended on me, and I had to learn to depend only on myself because I no longer had a partner.

My first big challenge came three weeks later when a pipe under the kitchen sink started leaking on a Sunday night. I had no idea what to do. Plumbing, or any type of household maintenance, is not my thing. I didn't even know how to shut off the water. Luckily, I had a friend who FaceTimed me, giving me specific instructions for how to make it stop. *Phew!* I was proud that I could stop my kitchen from flooding.

The plumbing issues continued. A toilet leaked and an upstairs bathtub leaked, causing damage to the ceiling below, and the hot water heater broke, creating a pond of water in the basement. My brother came to my rescue via FaceTime to show me how to use the shop vac.

After an hour of trying to clean up the puddles, I called him back because I thought there was something wrong with the equipment. As I held the phone up to the shop vac for him to check it out, he started laughing.

"What is it?" I asked.

"Debbie, you have the hose in there backwards," he replied.

I certainly wish I had called him sooner! As I continued sucking up the water, my shoe got stuck on a sticky mouse trap, and I lost it. I went from laughing at my stupidity to crying hysterically. *How am I going to be able to do all of this? Why did Gary have to leave me?* I had to walk away and take a break. One minute, you think you're so strong, and the next, you're consumed with grief.

With each mini disaster, my confidence grew. *I can do this.* I don't necessarily want to, but that really doesn't matter. We don't like everything we do every day, but this is part of life. It's part of being a functioning human. In addition to not knowing how to deal with maintenance issues, I also didn't know how to cook. Yes, you read that right. I was fifty-nine years old and had never cooked in my life.

I've always been a picky eater, so I never felt the need or desire to cook. My mom was a good cook, but the only time I wanted to be in the kitchen was when she was making brownies or cookies (which wasn't very often) so I could lick the beater. Once I lived on my own, I ate frozen dinners or would *conveniently* wind up at my mother's house at dinnertime. When Gary met me, he said the only things in my refrigerator were mustard, Diet Coke, and frozen Weight Watchers dinners. He was appalled.

He loved food, grocery shopping, and cooking. He was definitely the man for me! In the thirty years we were together, I barely stepped foot in a supermarket. It was fabulous. Once he became ill, I had no choice but to revert back to my old life and buy frozen dinners. We lived on frozen dinners and takeout.

After he died, I realized my kids and I needed to learn how to cook something other than microwave dinners. My friend Leslie took Ben, my youngest son, and me to two different supermarkets and gave us ideas on how to prepare a few easy meals. She then gave us hands-on instructions on how to actually cook something. Simultaneously, I purchased an air fryer so we could easily cook without the big mess and fuss.

For the first couple of months, it was fun to try new things. Ben experimented while Sam and I mostly stuck to the air fryer. Either way, all three of us felt empowered. Gary never wanted anyone in the kitchen with him, so the rest of us were oblivious to even the simplest things. Our meals were nowhere near as tasty as Gary's were, but we were doing it.

With each new challenge, my resilience and confidence grew. After sixty years of dealing with life's challenges, I know I can handle whatever life throws at me and eventually emerge with a positive outlook. However, it wasn't always this way. For years, I felt sorry for myself and wallowed in self-pity. I let the stress eat me up inside and was always on edge.

Over the past couple of years, I have discovered a tool that helps me deal with not only life-changing situations but everyday struggles as well. It's free-form journaling. I got comfortable with the journaling practice I learned in the first course I took, but that had prompts to answer; this was different. The idea is that you sit down and write without any agenda. You write anything that comes to mind. Some people set a timer, but I personally write until I feel I'm done. At first, the idea of doing this terrified me. *What the heck should I be writing about? Why did I need to write? Couldn't I just think about it as I've always done? What's the difference?*

I was actually afraid of a blank page. Maybe that sounds ridiculous, but I didn't like the idea of not having explicit instructions. The expectations were unclear, which made me anxious. One day I was listening to someone on a podcast discussing the benefits of this practice, which included stress reduction and helping to clarify your thoughts and feelings, so I decided it was worth a try.

At first, I was stumped. I had no idea what to write. I recalled the woman on the podcast saying if you don't know, then just keep writing, "I don't know what to write; I don't know what to write," and eventually something else will wind up on the page. She was certainly correct. I started and looked up fifteen minutes later. I was amazed at what came pouring out of me. It was astonishing. I started out writing about one thing, and by the time I finished, I had no idea how I wound up on that topic. It was incredibly therapeutic! I was hooked.

I have since added free-form journaling to my morning routine. Some days I don't have much to say and the session lasts five minutes, and others I'm shocked to learn what is really going on in my mind. Once again, I've found a tool I adore, one that would have stayed hidden in someone else's toolkit if I hadn't been open to changing my perspective and embracing new experiences.

Of course, there are many ways to build resilience. The first is making sure to take care of yourself. It seems obvious, but often we're so busy dealing firsthand with a situation or worrying that we forget or don't have time to pay attention to our own needs. Self-care comes in many different forms. It can be anything from spending time in nature to learning a new skill. Putting yourself first will allow you to handle whatever comes your way in a much calmer and more rational manner.

Reaching out to others for help and support and practicing gratitude and mindfulness are all ways to build resilience. None of us knows when we will need to call upon our resilience, but I want you to be as well prepared as possible. Building resilience doesn't happen overnight; it's a continuous process.

Remember, you are capable of more than you think. With each new challenge you overcome, you will not only survive but also thrive.

Remember, you are capable of more than you think. With each new challenge you overcome, you will not only survive but also thrive.

Key Takeaways:

1. Understanding Resilience: Resilience is our ability to bounce back from tough times. It helps us grow stronger and keep a positive outlook, no matter what we face.

2. Learning from Others: Just like Nelson Mandela's perseverance transformed his life and impacted the world, our struggles teach us valuable lessons about strength and courage.

3. It's a Journey: Building resilience doesn't happen overnight. It involves taking care of ourselves, reaching out for support, and finding tools like journaling to help us reflect and heal.

Activities

Activity 1: Free-form Journaling

Objective

Get out your thoughts and feelings in a safe way.

Instructions:

1. Write for a minimum of five minutes with no agenda. Use the trick I mentioned. If you don't know what to write, keep writing "I don't know what to write" until you eventually move on to something else.

2. Try this three to five times before deciding whether or not you find this tool useful. Many find it takes practice. Don't give up on the first go.

Activity 2: The Support Circle

Objective

Recognize and lean on your support network.

Instructions:

1. Make a list of people (family, friends, or community members) who have supported you in the past or whom you believe could support you now.

2. Next to each name, write down how they can help you (listening, advice, or practical help) and how you might reach out to them.

3. Commit to contacting at least one person from this list within the next week to seek support or simply connect.

Activity 3: Learning from Loss

Objective

Process feelings of loss and identify growth.

Instructions:

1. Reflect on a loss you have experienced and write about it, focusing not just on the pain but also on any growth or learning that came from it.

2. Identify specific strengths you discovered in yourself as a result of dealing with this loss.

3. Consider how you can apply these strengths in other areas of your life moving forward.

Journal Prompt

Reflect on your day-to-day activities. Identify a moment today where you demonstrated resilience, no matter how small the instance. How did it feel to persevere, and what did you learn about yourself?

13

A Sprinkle of Curiosity

LIME GREEN:
Fresh and zesty, lime green captures the essence of curiosity and the thirst for knowledge.

Shifting my mindset from "I can't" to "maybe I can" was life-changing. I opened myself up to new experiences, ideas, and people.

> **Shifting my mindset from "I can't" to "maybe I can" was life-changing.**

I saw the world with fresh eyes, anxious to learn all I could about anything that would help me on my life journey.

My exploration began with yoga after I lost the bulk of my weight. I had always enjoyed exercising, but I typically chose classes with a dance component to them. I assumed that yoga was for flexible people who looked good in leggings. That certainly wasn't me. When I was thirty-six years old, I had a spinal fusion, which means I have titanium screws and rods in my lower spine. In addition, I had two total hip replacements and sometimes still suffer from nerve pain.

I was under the care of a pain management specialist who told me for years I should be doing yoga and swimming, and I would tell him neither of those things were for me. With my mindset shift and the encouragement of a friend who was a yoga lover, I decided to give it a try. I went to a class at my gym, and although I didn't enjoy it and could barely keep up, I noticed my back felt better afterwards. I couldn't deny the fact that it helped, so I continued going to yoga classes at the gym once a week.

A new yoga studio opened around the block from my house, and my friend was one of their first customers. She loved it so much that she would go to a class almost every day. She urged me to give it a try. She particularly loved the hot yoga classes, and I was curious but completely intimidated. My limiting beliefs reminded me that I would be judged and embarrassed. However, I was able to turn off the voice, overcome my fear, and attend a hot yoga class.

Fifteen minutes into the class, I thought I would pass out from the heat and the speed and intensity of the poses. It was hard not to compare myself to my friend or the other students in the class. When we so-called "rested" in downward dog, I could barely "rest" without collapsing onto my mat. I don't know how, but I made it through the entire class, and when I was able to get outside and breathe some cool, fresh air, I was proud of myself.

I decided to try again, but this time I went alone and attended a gentle flow class, which was more my speed. Even though it was challenging, the benefits were hard to deny. My back felt better than it had in years, and I always left the studio feeling peaceful and relaxed. I took the plunge and became a member. After trying several classes and instructors, I settled on attending three days a week.

One day I overheard my friend talking about a five-thirty class she tried with an incredible instructor. I made a snarky comment, saying "It must be nice," because I couldn't get home from work in time to go to class. She then proceeded to put me in my place by letting me know the class wasn't at five-thirty in the afternoon but at five-thirty in the morning.

Gulp. I had no response and was ashamed of myself.

What choice did I have but to give it a try? When the alarm screeched at five o'clock in the morning, it took all the willpower I had not to turn it off and roll over, but I knew I was accountable to my friend, so I dragged myself into the bathroom, got dressed, and drove around the block in the pitch black to take a yoga class. There were only three other students in the class, which I wasn't sure if I liked. My inability to properly do the poses would be glaringly obvious.

As I struggled with a pose, the instructor quietly came over and whispered an alternative move for me to try. She helped guide my body into the pose with a kind smile on her face. My body happily complied and moved into position. I was sold. I became a regular early morning student and attended the three weekday classes. The class members developed a tight bond, and over time, the instructor morphed the class into something that worked for all of us by differentiating her instruction based on our skill level.

One morning, she announced that we were trying something new: adding a fifteen-minute meditation at the end of the class. Panic set in, recalling how I felt about savasana when I first took a yoga class at the gym. Savasana is typically the last pose of every class, where you lie on your back with your eyes closed and a relaxed body. Initially, it made me so uncomfortable to be sprawled out on my mat with my eyes closed in a room full of strangers.

What if everyone else was opening their eyes and looking at me? Judging me by how my body looked? I would lay there, my mind racing, waiting for the instructor to tell us to roll over, sit up, and end the class. *How did people find this relaxing? Maybe I could run out just before we assumed the position, so I wouldn't suffer.* I decided that would be worse, so I would lay there. Then one day, my voice began to quiet, and I realized how great it felt to lay there, feeling that sense of peace and release. Savasana soon became the pose I lived for.

However, you only lay in savasana for a couple of minutes, which is quite different from the fifteen minutes of meditation we were going to try. As we began by closing our eyes, I waited for the music to start, but it never did. It turns out that it was a silent meditation for fifteen minutes. *How the heck am I going to do this without music or talking?* The first five minutes or so were anxiety-filled, but then I was able to relax. My mind took me places that made no sense until I found myself singing silently "I Will Survive" by Gloria Gaynor, and tears streamed down my face. Life was very hard at that time, and the song was a message to me.

What else could it be? I hadn't heard or thought about that song in years. I couldn't wait for the meditation to end so I could share my experience with the others. I surprised myself with my ability to actually do it. I was able to sit quietly for fifteen minutes with my eyes closed. I didn't jump out of my skin or dash out the front door. Look at what I discovered! I couldn't wait to try again.

Prior to the class meditation, I had experimented with different meditation apps. I searched for that sense of calm and peace. I needed something to help combat the constant stress I felt, and I was curious to learn what all the hype was about. I found that I preferred a guided meditation where someone talks me through it, reminding me to return to my breath when my mind wanders off. I worked my way up to ten minutes at a time after starting at one minute.

I began to crave this quiet time and wanted to learn more, so I attended a private training in transcendental meditation. In this type of meditation, each individual is given a mantra that is personally chosen for them, and it's not to be shared with anyone else. At a minimum, you are supposed to practice twice a day for at least twenty minutes at a time. The morning was easy for me; however, I had difficulty incorporating it into my evenings.

After the initial private training, I attended group Zoom calls where we would have a short lesson and meditate together. My yoga teacher primed me for this since I was used to fifteen minutes of silence. *What's another five minutes? I have become a meditator!* It only happened because I persevered. I didn't allow the discomfort to stop me.

It only happened because I persevered. I didn't allow the discomfort to stop me.

When you try out new things like yoga and meditation, you're tapping into some serious science that shows how good they are for your mind and body. Take the Mindfulness-Based Stress Reduction (MBSR) program originally created by Dr. Jon Kabat-Zinn at the University of Massachusetts Medical Center, for instance. People who went through this program found they were way less stressed, could handle their emotions better, and felt healthier mentally. This stuff works because it actually changes parts of your brain that help you remember better, feel more for others, and stay calm under pressure.

What else is out there? My mind was now open to exploring.

I was already a big fan of Reiki, which is an energy healing technique where a Reiki Master guides the flow of healthy energy through your body by using very light touch. I found it very relaxing and never wanted my sessions to end. It was odd at first, but once I was able to stop my mind from telling me how weird this was, I really enjoyed it.

Sound healing also became a new favorite of mine. You lay on your mat with your eyes closed while your guide plays a variety of sounds and music using different sound-healing instruments. I found it to be powerful and meditative. Unfortunately, the in-person classes aren't held too often where I live.

My exploration continued, and I learned a tiny bit about things I had never heard of before, such as:

Human Design: This system combines principles from astrology, I Ching, Kabbalah, and the chakra system to create a unique personality map for an individual. This map, known as a BodyGraph, is supposed to reveal how a person is designed to navigate life, make decisions, and interact with others based on their specific date, time, and place of birth.

Neuro-Linguistic Programming (NLP): This psychological approach involves understanding and using the language of the mind to consistently achieve specific, desired outcomes. It combines techniques from cognitive and behavioral psychology and is often used in therapy, coaching, and communication training to help individuals change their thoughts and behaviors.

Somatic Breathwork: There are many different types of breathwork; this is just one example. Somatic breathwork is a type of breathing practice that emphasizes the connection between the breath and the physical body. It focuses on using breath to release tension, manage stress, and enhance bodily awareness. The individual is guided to notice sensations in the body while breathing in specific patterns, which can help to identify and release areas of physical tension or emotional blockages. The goal is to bring about a state of greater physical relaxation and psychological balance by allowing the body to naturally regulate and heal itself.

Tai Chi: This traditional Chinese martial art combines deep breathing and relaxation with slow, gentle movements. It is practiced both as a form of meditation and for its health benefits, such as improving balance, flexibility, and overall physical and mental well-being.

Enneagram: This system categorizes people into nine different personality types. Each type is based on specific motivations and fears. It is often used to help people understand themselves better and improve their personal growth.

Emotional Freedom Technique (EFT): This therapeutic method combines elements of acupressure and psychology. It involves tapping specific points on the body with the fingertips while focusing on and verbalizing emotional issues. This practice is intended to help reduce emotional distress and promote a deeper sense of peace and well-being.

Crystal Therapy: This alternative healing uses crystals and gemstones to promote physical and emotional healing. Practitioners believe crystals have natural energy properties that can interact with the body's energy field to improve balance and wellness.

Forest Bathing: The practice of spending time in a forest enhances health, wellness, and happiness. The idea is to connect with nature through the senses to reduce stress and improve overall well-being.

Was I dropped into an alternate universe? I was discovering there was an entire world out there that I knew nothing about. Not everything I tried was for me, but that was okay, and it won't be for you either. It doesn't matter, though, because it was interesting and stimulating, shifting my outlook on life. Each morning, I woke up excited about the day, looking forward to experiencing and learning new things.

All those preconceived notions I had disappeared. I saw firsthand how many of those beliefs came from a place of ignorance and fear. Curiosity opens up new opportunities, making life richer and more interesting. So drop all those assumptions, biases, and judgments and get out there and be curious. Open yourself up to something new today—maybe it's a book from a genre you've never touched or a class you've been curious about. You don't need to leap; just take one small step. Who knows? It might be the beginning of your own beautiful journey towards a more curious and fulfilling life, leading you to amazing places.

Key Takeaways:

1. Try New Things: Jumping into new activities, even if they feel a bit out of reach, can really boost both your physical and mental well-being. For example, starting yoga might be tough at first, but the benefits for your back and peace of mind can be undeniable.

2. Let Curiosity Lead: Allowing your curiosity to guide you can open up a world of new experiences, enriching your life significantly. Whether it's a new hobby or cultural exploration, it makes every day more exciting and fulfilling.

3. Face Your Fears: By actively engaging in new experiences, you'll start to dismantle your fears and build real confidence. From experimenting with different healing techniques to exploring philosophical ideas, taking these steps can transform your outlook and strengthen your spirit.

Curiosity opens up new opportunities, making life richer and more interesting.

Activities

Activity 1: Curiosity Quest

Objective

Embark on a journey of discovery, exploring new hobbies, practices, or knowledge areas.

Instructions:

1. List five activities or subjects you've always been curious about but haven't explored. These could range from artistic endeavors like painting or writing, to physical activities such as yoga or hiking, to academic interests like learning a new language or exploring astronomy.

2. Choose one from your list and commit to trying it out within the next month.

3. Research local classes, online tutorials, or simply start with books from the library.

4. Journal about your experience, noting how it felt to try something new, what you learned, and whether it's something you'd like to continue.

Activity 2: Daily Wonder Walk

Objective

Cultivate mindfulness and an observant eye towards the everyday world.

Instructions:

1. Take a daily walk, but with the specific intention of noticing five new things you haven't seen before. These could be as simple as the color of a neighbor's door, a plant growing through a crack in the sidewalk, or the way the light casts shadows at a certain time of day.

2. After your walk, spend a few minutes writing about these observations and how they might relate to the broader world or your inner life.

Activity 3: Idea Exploration Journal

Objective

Create a dedicated space for exploring new ideas and reflections.

Instructions:

1. Start an "Idea Exploration Journal." This can be a physical notebook or a digital document, whatever feels most comfortable and accessible.

2. Whenever you encounter a new idea that sparks interest—whether from a book, conversation, podcast, etc.—make a note of it in your journal. Write down why it intrigues you and how you might explore it further.

3. Commit to revisiting one of these ideas each week, dedicating time to learning more about it through further research, experimentation, or reflection.

Journal Prompt

Reflect on what fascinated you as a child. Are there elements of those early curiosities that you still find intriguing today? How can you reconnect with those interests now?

14

A Sprinkle of Connection

PINK:
Warm and inviting, pink is ideal for the nurturing aspect of connection.

My friends describe me as a "groupoholic." I absolutely love being a part of a group, particularly a group of people who share a common interest or challenge. There's something about the camaraderie and energy. Maybe it began with playing on softball teams at an early age. Working together for a common goal was powerful, and we all needed to rely on one another.

It's no coincidence that the diet I was most successful with was Weight Watchers. Many people didn't want to attend the meetings each week, but for me, that was the best part. I was inspired by others' stories of success and could relate when they spoke of their struggles. It took me years to work up enough courage to participate since I had a lifelong fear of being judged; however, once I saw how safe the environment was, I spoke up. Once I did, it made the meeting all the more impactful, as people offered words of encouragement or praise. It helped create and strengthen my relationships with other members as we learned more about one another.

Similarly, I've found great comfort in other types of support groups. When Sam was diagnosed as a toddler with autism spectrum disorder, I connected with other moms and attended a support group. These were the only people who could truly understand what I was going through. The judgmental looks I would get from strangers when Sam acted out in public made me want to scream. It was obvious they had determined I was a bad mother because my child was having a temper tantrum, particularly as he got older. The opportunity to share that with other moms who said, "Me, too!" made me feel like I wasn't alone.

Years later, when both Sam and Gary were struggling with mental illness, I joined a support group through NAMI (National Alliance for Mental Illness) for family members of those with mental illness. This was truly a safe space where we could all share candidly. Mental illness is an incredibly difficult disease to treat and understand unless you're living with it every day. In addition to sharing my own experiences, I always walked away with an untapped resource. Navigating this world is confusing and challenging, so the information they shared was invaluable.

Professionally, groups have played a tremendous role in my life and progress. When I became an insurance agent and was going through the training and trial period, I was surrounded by others in the same boat. We supported and helped one another, and thirty years later, several of them are still close friends. I became an author with the support of a group for first-time writers. They helped hold me accountable in a very loving and non-judgmental way. Sharing ideas and struggles made it feel like we were doing this together. I honestly don't think you would be reading this right now if it weren't for them.

Conversely, have you ever been around people who make you feel crummy? Early in my insurance career, I sampled different networking groups and found that I didn't like most of them. In fact, I wanted to turn around and run right out of the room after ten minutes and would have done so if no one would have noticed. There was an air of superiority and selfishness in those meetings. People were only there to sell you themselves and their services. Of course, that's what networking is all about; however, if you are with the right people, they are genuinely there to form relationships.

Or think about when you meet someone and there's just something about them that brings you down. Maybe all they do is complain or make a negative comment about anything you say. How does that make you feel? I feel like I need to take a shower after being in the presence of someone like that. I want to wash away all that negativity. For many years, I didn't realize how big of an impact those around me had on my life.

When my boys were younger, I felt like I was back in school again, trying to get in with the cool crowd. When Sam was in preschool and even kindergarten, most of the moms included Sam and me in their playdates and birthday parties. However, as he got older, that came to a screeching halt. Sam had trouble with transitions, loud noises, and playing appropriately, so as the other kids grew older, they no longer looked at him as a suitable playmate. This, in turn, meant I was out as well.

When Ben came along, I was able to hang in there a little longer. He had his own set of issues, as all of us do, but the others would still play with him. As he got older and sports became the main form of socializing, things changed. Ben was a good athlete, but he was not great, and many of his friends seemed to fall into the great category. Ben was the star on the "B" team but would become the bench warmer if he happened to make it onto the "A" team.

This meant that on weekends, all his friends' parents were hanging out together at the ballfields of the "A" team and we were not. When he was lucky enough to make the "A" team, he was not viewed as a productive member of the team. It would make me uncomfortable, as I felt the others would judge or be annoyed if Ben didn't perform to their liking. Even so, I still wanted to be part of the "A" team moms.

When I was included and we went out to dinner or hung out at someone's home, I hated it. I had nothing in common with these women, and I only enjoyed the company of a select few. After a night with them, I would come home feeling depressed. The talk was about their talented children or some other aspect of their perfect lives. However, I thought the problem was me. I didn't give birth to the kids that fit in. *What else is new?* I still longed to be included as a part of this club.

It wasn't until Ben was a preteen that I saw the correlation between hanging with this group and my moods. It was crazy because I didn't even enjoy their company. *Why on earth would I want to waste my precious time with this group when I always left feeling badly about myself and defeated?* I realized I had to let this obsession with fitting in go. Who in their right mind craves a social connection like this? Maybe kids and teens, but I was a grown woman in my early fifties.

It was still tough the first time I turned down an invitation. I wasn't perfect and still occasionally attended. However, each time I wasn't strong enough and participated, I saw how socializing with this group was ridiculous. It has taken me years to learn to say no to spending time with people who don't make me feel good. As a people-pleaser and social person, turning down invitations is difficult, but all it takes is one night with someone who leaves me feeling down to remind me that the word "no" is a powerful tool.

According to Jim Rohn, "You are the average of the five people you spend the most time with." Meaning, the people you surround yourself with shape your life and your future. Think about it: If you're surrounded by people who have a negative outlook and only talk about all that is wrong in the world and how unfair life is, it will be difficult for you to have a positive view of life. On the other hand, if you're trying to attain a goal and are spending time with high achievers who you find inspirational and are cheering you on, chances are you will succeed.

> **According to Jim Rohn, "you are the average of the five people you spend the most time with." The people you surround yourself with shape your life and your future.**

Having a group of friends who share your values, interests, and support your growth can literally change your life.
The right community can offer encouragement, accountability, and a sense of belonging.

Having a group of friends who share your values and interests and support your growth can literally change your life. The right community can offer encouragement, accountability, and a sense of belonging. So how do you find these people? You have to be willing to search for them by attending different groups and events. It could be things like book clubs, a meetup, or a seminar. Maybe you volunteer or join a professional organization. You could also join an online group or start your own if you can't find what you are looking for.

To me, the more difficult problem is figuring out how to deal with friends and family who don't align with you. Cutting them out of your life is not necessary; however, it is important to have some guidelines when it comes to your relationship. The first thing to do is to set boundaries. Let them know that there are some topics you don't want to discuss. Instead, try to focus on your shared interests.

As in any relationship, keeping the lines of communication open is important. Help them understand your perspective and why you're engaging in certain activities. If they truly care about you, they will respect your boundaries and choices, even if they don't fully understand or share your interests. On the other hand, it's also crucial to respect their perspectives and boundaries, ensuring that mutual respect is maintained in the relationship.

Another important strategy is to diversify your social circles. You don't need to rely on a single group of people for all your social and emotional needs. Having a variety of friends and acquaintances allows you to enjoy different aspects of your personality and interests with different groups. This way, you can engage deeply in your passions with like-minded individuals without straining other valuable relationships that might not share those specific interests.

Finally, always make room for personal growth and the re-evaluation of your relationships. People change, and so do their interests and values. Regularly taking stock of your relationships to ensure they are still positive and supportive is essential. This doesn't always mean cutting ties, but it might mean adjusting the amount of time you spend with certain people or how you interact with them to better serve your well-being and personal growth goals.

By consciously choosing who you spend time with and how you interact with them, you will create a supportive network that fosters personal development and happiness while also maintaining a healthy balance with those who may not entirely align with your current path.

Key Takeaways:

1. Strength In Community: Being part of groups like Weight Watchers or a support group for parents of children with autism shows how shared challenges can bring people together, offering support and inspiration.

2. Choose Your Circle Wisely: The people you hang out with can really shape your life. Spending time with positive folks can boost your mood and help you reach your goals.

3. Setting Boundaries: It's okay to have limits with friends and family who don't see eye-to-eye with you. Clear boundaries help keep these relationships healthy without stopping your personal progress.

Activities

Activity 1: Connecting with New People

Objective
Identify people you've wanted to meet but have been hesitant to approach, and create a simple plan to connect with them.

Step 1: Reflect on Your Current Circle

List Five People: Who do you spend the most time with? Next to each name, note if they uplift or drain you.

Step 2: Identify Potential Connections

List New People: Write down the names of people you want to meet and why you're interested in them.

Step 3: Face Your Fears

Note the Hesitation: Write down what has stopped you from reaching out to each person in the past.

Challenge the Fear: Counter each fear with a positive thought.

Step 4: Make a Plan

Choose Your Method: Decide how you'll reach out—call, email, or in person.

Draft your Message: Keep it simple and genuine. Set a Deadline: Pick a date to reach out by.

Step 5: Reflect on the Outcome

Note the Experience: How did it go? What did you learn? Adjust if Needed: If it didn't go as planned, think about how to improve next time.

Activity 2: Community Exploration Exercise

Objective

Physically connect with communities that share your interests or values, enriching your social life and expanding your network.

Instructions:

1. Research local clubs, organizations, or groups that align with your interests. You can use online resources, community boards, or local event listings.

2. Make a list of these groups, noting down contact information and meeting times.

3. Choose one group from your list and commit to attending a meeting or event within the next month.

4. Prepare a few questions or topics of discussion for when you attend to ensure you engage actively.

5. Reflect on your experience afterwards to determine if this group feels like a good fit for your personal and social growth.

Activity 3: Join Online Forums

Objective
Digitally engage with communities that share your interests, providing you with a platform to learn, share, and grow.

Instructions:

1. Identify online forums, social media groups, or platforms that focus on your areas of interest.

2. Create an account on one or more of these platforms if you haven't already.

3. Start by reading existing discussions to get a feel for the community's tone and topics.

4. Actively participate by posting your own insights, responding to others' posts, or asking questions. Aim to make at least one post and two comments in your first week.

5. Evaluate after a week if your chosen platforms add value to your knowledge and whether the community engagement is beneficial to your growth.

Journal Prompt

Reflect on a time when being part of a group or community had a positive impact on your life. What did you gain from that experience?

15

A Sprinkle of Joy

YELLOW:
Often seen as bright, cheerful, and uplifting, yellow symbolizes happiness, positivity, and warmth.

I used to roll my eyes at the idea of gratitude journals and daily affirmations. It all seemed like fluff to me. I remember the first time I attended an online business mastermind meeting, a group where business owners share ideas and support each other, and the facilitators instructed us to tell everyone what we were grateful for before posing our question to the group. *What kind of nonsense is this? What is the point?* I decided it was the leaders adding filler in order to waste some time. Of course, I don't think I ever asked a question because I was too intimidated, so I never had to be concerned about playing the gratitude game.

As I listened to more podcasts and read more books, I found that gratitude seemed to be a recurrent theme. *Is this gratitude stuff something the entire personal development industry has bought into?* I didn't get it. *I mean, isn't it obvious that I'm grateful for my friends and family, my house, my health, etc.? What's the point of saying it out loud?* I decided to chalk it up to some woo-woo stuff that logically made no sense, at least not to me.

My attitude changed when Shana, my business coach, sent me a gratitude journal as a gift. She was forcing the issue. *Seriously? Now I have no choice but to fill this thing out.* It was so thoughtful of her to send it to me, so putting the journal on the shelf to collect dust was not an option. As I cracked open the book to see what was inside, my eyes did a roll that said it all. *Oh brother!*

Each day had two pages, one for the morning and another for the night. It was bad enough that I had to fill this thing out once a day, but twice? Here are the prompts from the journal:

Morning Meditation:

1. Today's focus

2. An affirmation for today

3. What I'm grateful for

4. What I'm excited about today

5. How I'll make space for gratitude today

Evening Reflection:

1. Good things that happened today

2. Things I did to make a positive difference today

3. How I felt today (there was a checklist of different feelings where you could check off boxes)

4. A positive thought to carry me to sleep

I decided the best way to make sure I used the journal was to habit stack. Habit stacking is the idea that you pair the new habit you're cultivating with a habit that's already part of your regular routine. I already had a consistent morning routine, so I decided I would fill out the journal each day after I meditated.

Some of my answers were similar day after day, which made me think I was doing it all wrong. I put pressure on myself, like I was turning my journal in for a grade from the gratitude teacher. I knew I had to let go of this story and tell myself a better one, so I gave myself permission to write the same exact thing each and every day. No big deal.

I struggled with the daily affirmation section because I had absolutely no idea what I should be writing, so I decided to choose one each day from a list I either found online or from suggestions I still had from the original mindset course I took. Here are some of my affirmation entries:

I am welcoming all the ways the universe wants to bless me.

I am creating the life of my dreams.

I am learning to be grateful for what I have while being excited for what has yet to come.

Money flows to me easily and often.

I have everything I need within me to manifest all that I desire.

I am passionate about my goals and have a burning desire to fulfill them.

Everything is always working out for me.

I can't miss what's meant for me.

And last but not least, the only one that I created, although I know I heard it somewhere else first: *This is my one and only life!* I wanted to keep reminding myself that this is my one shot, and since I made the decision to turn this ship around, I needed to stay focused on my "why" and my goals.

I actually found answering the prompt, "What I'm excited about today," helpful. It made me reflect on the upcoming events and realize there was always something to look forward to. It was nice to spend time thinking about good things instead of only thinking about what I dreaded.

Initially, I listed the same things under the "What I'm grateful for" category. However, my mind soon wandered in ways it had not before as I went through my day. When I walked Yogi, my maltipoo, instead of looking at my phone, I paid attention to the world around me. I noticed the leaves on the trees swaying back and forth, the beautiful view right outside my front door, and the birds chirping as they flew overhead.

Now, just to be clear, I have never been someone who appreciates nature. I couldn't fathom why people would hike, camp, and be outside with bugs and critters. I was not that person. Gary used to sit on our front porch for hours watching the squirrels, birds, and bees. For the first couple of years we were together, he would ask me to sit out there with him, but I was always too busy, so he eventually stopped asking. I would shake my head at him because I viewed what he was doing as a waste of time and lazy. Boy, was I an idiot!

The entries in my journal began to change. Here are some of my entries about things I was grateful for:

The moon

Colored pens

Cold, calm, fresh air
A quiet house
My ability to change my mindset
Yogi, laying by my side
Zoom

Each time I identified something else I was grateful for, my mood improved and a smile appeared on my face. I started to buy into this gratitude thing. I couldn't believe there was really something to it. My focus shifted from all the things I lacked to realizing just how lucky I actually was.

> **My focus shifted from all the things I lacked to realizing just how lucky I actually was.**

Now I didn't walk around telling everyone how grateful I was for the moon and the stars in the sky, but I did try telling the people in my life how I felt. Even if it wasn't with words but with a smile or hug. I'm not just talking about my close family and friends; I felt gratitude towards the woman at the McDonald's drive thru where I went every day to get my morning Diet Coke, the young man at the pharmacy, and my 6 a.m. workout buddies. Experiencing the joy of making someone else feel good inspired me to seek out more opportunities to spread happiness.

There's actual science behind this phenomenon. In 2003, the study "Counting blessings versus burdens: An experimental investigation of gratitude and subjective well-being in daily life" found that gratitude may improve psychological well-being. Its leading psychologist, Dr. Emmons said, "Gratitude heals, energizes and changes lives. It is the prism through which we view life in terms of gifts, givers, goodness and grace." This landmark study has inspired many others over the years. A study published in the National Library of Medicine in March 2018, "Does gratitude writing improve the mental health of psychotherapy clients? Evidence from a randomized controlled trial," explored the concept further. The research team found people who practice gratitude experience reduced symptoms of anxiety and depression, increased self-esteem, and more satisfaction with life.

There's actual science behind this practice, which I had resisted.

Getting back to my journal, I have to be honest and tell you that I consistently filled out the journal in the morning but not so much in the evening. I decided that I would keep a pen on my nightstand, completing the journal before I turned out the light while in bed. The big snag was that I filled out the journal downstairs in the morning, and my bedroom was upstairs. I had to remember to bring the journal upstairs at night. I tried to remember to leave it out in the morning so it was visible in the evening, but that didn't seem to work. Often, I'd be focused on carrying other things upstairs and forget. Once I was upstairs, if I remembered, I was too lazy to get it.

Since that strategy wasn't working, I tried bringing it upstairs in the morning after I filled it out. I would usually be heading up to take a shower. The problem then became that I forgot to fill out the journal in the morning because it was upstairs. *Ugh!* Then I tried filling it out downstairs before I went up to bed, which would work occasionally. In the end, I took the pressure off myself, satisfied with just my morning practice. I reminded myself that there is no right or wrong with gratitude; it's whatever works for me.

An easy way to start is by thinking of three things you're grateful for before getting out of bed in the morning, although that doesn't work for me because the minute I open my eyes, I need to get to the bathroom to pee *stat* (too much information?)! It might be easier, if you have a bladder like mine, to practice at night when you get into bed. Other people create a gratitude jar, and each time they are grateful for something or someone, they jot it down on a piece of paper and put it in the jar. When life gets you down, reading those slips of paper can be a great way to get those negative thoughts out of your head.

I started to take notice of all the little things in my life that made me smile. I've always had a little girl inside of me who still loved Mickey Mouse, hearts, and my birthday. I was intentional about making sure there were little reminders of those things in all the spaces in my home and office where I spent time because they made me feel good. One night, a couple of months before Gary died, I was shopping on my phone. I was looking for a shirt, and in the search bar, I typed the word "hearts," which wasn't unusual for me. As I hit the enter button, a vision appeared in my mind.

An easy way to start is by thinking of three things you're grateful for before getting out of bed in the morning.

It was a picture of a store in Washington, D.C. that only sold items with hearts on them. I discovered it when I was in college and became obsessed with it. I wanted to visit the store and browse any chance I could get. My friends grew tired of me begging them to hop on the metro to head down there every weekend. Just walking through the doors of that store gave me a sense of complete and utter joy. I longed to be locked in there overnight and sleep there so I could soak up that feeling and keep it with me.

I fantasized back then and told my friend Mary that someday I would own a heart store. It might be this one, or I would open up one of my own in New York. I was serious. I wanted to capture that joy and never let it go. I wanted to pass the joy onto others and make other people break into a smile that they felt from their head to their toes. I just needed to graduate college and earn enough money to get it started.

Of course, after graduation, I got a job as an accountant since that was what my degree was in, and eventually my dream faded from my mind until that night, shopping in my bed. I realized that it was 2022, and that meant you no longer needed a brick-and-mortar store to own a business. I could open my heart store online, but I had absolutely no idea how to go about doing that.

Luckily, through the mastermind I attended, I met a wonderful woman who helped people start online businesses. This was a woman I liked, respected, and trusted, so I hopped on a Zoom call with her and told her my predicament. My husband was dying, I was writing a book, and I had no money or time. "So do you think I could make this work?" I asked, laughing. She explained my options and cost, and the next thing I knew, I was opening a store.

Working on opening the store over the next few weeks gave me that feeling I experienced forty years earlier. I couldn't wait to bring this to life and share my joy with others. Of course, there were days when I thought I had completely lost my mind taking on something else at a time like this, but then I would remind myself that I was fulfilling a long-lost dream. I couldn't stop now.

My goal was to have the store up and running on January 14, 2023, exactly one month before Valentine's Day. It turned out that was also the day that I committed to turning the first draft of my memoir into the editor. When Gary died on December 30, 2022, all my plans were put on hold until after the funeral was over and all my friends and relatives returned to their regular lives.

I sat there alone in my home office, contemplating how I could possibly concentrate on both these monumental goals in the next week. Writing had helped me through some very tough times over the past few months, so focusing would certainly help me as I tried to digest the fact that I was a widow. I knew I needed to stick to my original plan. My cousin Mindy and I visited the Museum of Ice Cream in New York City along with a photographer. The plan was to take pictures of me for my heart store website. You see, something else that brings me great happiness is ice cream with rainbow sprinkles. This is why I named my online store A Sprinkle of Hearts.

Who even knew the Museum of Ice Cream was a real thing? You walk through rooms with fun and different photo opportunities, and along the way you're served ice cream. How great is that? I loved it and had so much fun. The grand finale is a pool of sprinkles that you can jump into. Just for the record, they aren't real sprinkles, but Styrofoam ones.

It was like being in a ball pit, and I reveled in lying there, throwing the sprinkles in the air. All my worries were replaced with the carefree feeling of being a child again. The photographer successfully captured my joy, and the picture went onto my store website, www.ASprinkleOfHearts.com.

On launch day, I proudly scrolled through all the selections I shared with the rest of the world. I found my own joy by bringing joy to others. There was no better feeling in the world!

Embracing gratitude turned out to be more than just a trendy practice—it really changed my life. At first, I thought it was all fluff, but the more I journaled, the more I noticed and appreciated the little things around me. This small act of writing down what I was thankful for each day shifted my outlook and made me happier. It's amazing how a simple habit like gratitude can open your eyes to the joys often overlooked. So, from someone who once doubted it, I can say gratitude really does work—it makes life richer and more fulfilling.

> **So, from someone who once doubted it, I can say gratitude really does work—it makes life richer and more fulfilling.**

I encourage you to give gratitude a chance, even if it feels a bit odd at first. Start small, maybe with a quiet moment of thanks each morning, and watch how it transforms your outlook. You might just find yourself smiling more often, feeling lighter, and perhaps even spreading that joy to others. Remember, the best parts of life might be sprinkled in the simplest moments.

> **Key Takeaways:**
>
> 1. Gratitude Reveals Hidden Joys: The practice of gratitude can lead to the discovery of joy in unexpected places. By focusing on what you're thankful for, you may start to notice the small, often overlooked details in your daily life that bring happiness, leading to a deeper appreciation for the present moment.
>
> 2. Gratitude Can Change Your Outlook: Even if you're skeptical at first, regularly writing down what you're thankful for can transform your outlook. It turns out that noticing and appreciating the simple things can make life feel richer and more enjoyable.
>
> 3. Spreading Gratitude Feels Great: Sharing your gratitude isn't just good for you; it lifts others up, too. Whether it's a smile, a thank you, or a kind note, showing gratitude makes a big difference in your community and circles.

Activities

Activity 1: Gratitude Morning Kick-off

Objective

Begin each day with a mindset focused on gratitude, positively impacting your mood and outlook.

Instructions:

1. Each morning, before getting out of bed or while in the bathroom, mentally list three things you're grateful for. These can be as simple as the comfort of your bed, the sunshine peeking through your window, or a specific person in your life.

2. Reflect on why each of these things brings you joy or comfort, delving a bit deeper into the feeling of gratitude.

Activity 2: Happiness Habit Tracker

Objective

Identify and cultivate personal habits that contribute to your happiness.

Instructions:

1. Create a list of activities that make you feel happy and fulfilled. Include both simple, daily activities and more significant, less frequent ones.

2. Use a habit tracker (either a physical tracker in a planner or a digital app) to monitor how often you engage in these happiness-boosting activities. Aim to incorporate at least one into your daily routine.

Activity 3: Acts of Kindness Day

Objective

Experience the joy of giving through random acts of kindness.

Instructions:

1. Designate one day each month as your "Acts of Kindness Day." Plan ahead by listing acts of kindness you can easily carry out, such as leaving a positive note for someone, paying for the person behind you in line at the coffee shop, or donating to a local charity.

2. Reflect on how each act of kindness made you feel and the reactions you received. This can further cement the positive impact such actions have on your own sense of well-being.

Journal Prompt

Reflect on a recent moment that brought you pure joy. What was happening, and how did it make you feel?

Conclusion

A Sprinkle of New Beginnings

RAINBOW:
Ultimately, joy encompasses all the colors, reflecting a life lived with happiness and vibrancy.

This book might be ending, but your journey has just begun.

Remember where you started—feeling like life was passing you by, caught on that hamster wheel, and unhappy with the way things had turned out. Just as I once did, you may have felt exhausted, overwhelmed, and resigned to a life you didn't choose. But now, you've discovered the power within yourself to change.

This is your one and only life. You deserve to live it as you see fit, regardless of the circumstances and people around you. It won't happen by chance; you need to be intentional. It will be challenging, but you will persevere because you're worth it! Today is the day you draw a line in the sand, just as I did when I turned fifty.

It's a new beginning.

Your jar of sprinkles is now full. You have every color of the rainbow and more. Now it's up to you whether you put the jar away in a cabinet rarely to be seen or keep it on your counter and use it daily. This book is only the beginning of your new, vibrant, and extraordinary life. It has set you on a journey of self-discovery that must continue.

Where do you want to go from here? Do you want to learn more about mindsets and add more blue sprinkles to your life? If so, continue your exploration, since this book only scratches the surface. There are other sprinkles we didn't explore that you might want to add to your jar, such as a sprinkle of patience, peace, or creativity. Maybe scratch that—just in case I write part two! (LOL!)

Now that you've come to the end of this book, I'd like you to make sure you have all the sprinkles in your jar we explored. Here's a recap:

1. Perspective (Blue)

> Perspective Shapes Our Reality: Changing how we view our roles and responsibilities can profoundly impact our happiness and effectiveness.
>
> Embracing Different Viewpoints: Recognizing that others may have valid perspectives can broaden our understanding and enrich our interactions.
>
> Openness to New Perspectives Is Key: Being willing to reconsider our viewpoints can lead to significant personal growth and improved relationships.

2. Mindset (Silver)

> Transformative Power of Mindset: Shifting from a fixed to a growth mindset expands possibilities and impacts outcomes.

Challenges as Growth Opportunities: Embrace challenges as chances to learn and grow, not just obstacles.

Importance of Self-Awareness: Use tools like journaling and mindfulness to increase self-awareness and guide your mindset transformation.

3. Belief (Gold)

Spotting Limiting Beliefs: The reasons we often doubt ourselves, like feeling scared or not good enough, develop early and stem from what we learn from parents, teachers, and friends.

Changing Our Brain: Our brain can learn new ways of thinking, which means we can change old doubts into positive thoughts that help us do better.

Being Honest with Ourselves: It is important to pay attention to our own thoughts and actively change the negative ones so we can truly achieve what we're capable of.

4. Courage (Red)

Fear Is Natural; Courage Is a Choice: Embrace fear as a part of life, but recognize that stepping beyond it to pursue new opportunities is where true growth and transformation happen.

Small Acts of Courage Build Confidence: Regularly facing fears, even in small ways, strengthens your confidence and proves to yourself that you can handle challenges.

Growth Through Discomfort: Stepping out of your comfort zone is essential for personal development and achieving your full potential.

5. Responsibility (Green)

Control Your Reactions: The formula E + R = O (Event + Response = Outcome) shows us that our power lies in how we respond, not just in what happens to us. By focusing on our reactions, we can truly influence the results.

Stepping Up to the Plate: Realizing that you have a hand in the outcomes of your life through how you respond to events is crucial. It's about owning up to the fact that you're not a passive observer but an active participant in your story.

Owning Your Choices: Taking responsibility means recognizing that you hold the steering wheel in your life's journey. This realization is empowering, giving you the freedom to navigate life's ups and downs with confidence and purpose.

6. Dreams (Purple)

Let Yourself Dream: Don't hold back—imagine the biggest, boldest life you can. Believing in your dreams is the first step to making them come true.

Your Attitude Matters: How you react to what life throws at you shapes where you end up. Stay positive and see challenges as opportunities to grow.

Act on Your Dreams: Hope isn't just wishful thinking; it's a call to action. Start small, keep at it, and those big dreams will start to feel a lot closer.

7. Direction (Orange)

Set S.M.A.R.T. Goals: Ensure your goals are specific, measurable, achievable, relevant, and time-bound to increase the likelihood of success.

Break It Down: Divide your ultimate goals into smaller, manageable steps to prevent feeling overwhelmed and to make progress more achievable.

Stay Consistent: Consistency is key to achieving goals. Start with small steps and maintain a steady effort to gradually build toward your larger aspirations.

8. Vision (Violet)

Picture Success: Visualization helps you see yourself achieving your goals, just like athletes do before a big game.

Use Your Senses: Make your mental movies vivid by imagining what you see, hear, and feel. The more detailed, the better!

Practice Regularly: Like any skill, the more you practice visualization, the better you get. Make it a habit to visualize your goals often for maximum impact.

9. Action (Magenta)

Start Small: Tackle your goals with small, manageable steps. This makes the process less daunting and helps you get going without feeling overwhelmed.

Face Your Fears: Don't let the fear of messing up hold you back. Remember, taking action is always better than doing nothing. Every step forward is progress.

Stay Consistent: Keep at it, even if the steps are tiny. Regular effort adds up, turning small actions into big achievements over time. It's all about keeping the momentum going!

10. Discipline (Gray)

Find Your Why: Understanding your deeper motivation helps sustain discipline. Knowing why you're pursuing a goal provides clarity and fuels your perseverance, especially when challenges arise.

Set Up Routines: A consistent routine can be a game-changer. It puts you in control and sets the tone for a productive day, helping you stick to your plan and move closer to your goals.

Seek Support: Don't do it alone! Finding someone to share your journey with can make a huge difference. An accountability partner not only motivates you but also celebrates your successes and supports you through challenges.

11. Adaptability (Teal)

Embrace Flexibility: Life's unexpected challenges are opportunities to learn and grow. Being flexible allows you to navigate these challenges effectively, continually progressing towards your goals.

Reframe Setbacks as Lessons: Like Thomas Edison's approach to inventing the light bulb, view each setback as a step closer to success, not as a failure. This mindset transforms obstacles into steppingstones.

Adaptability Is Essential for Growth: Constantly evaluate and adjust your strategies in response to life's changes. This adaptability not only helps in overcoming obstacles but also in seizing new opportunities that arise.

12. Resilience (Indigo)

Understanding Resilience: Resilience is our ability to bounce back from tough times. It helps us grow stronger and keep a positive outlook, no matter what we face.

Learning from Others: Just like Nelson Mandela's perseverance transformed his life and impacted the world, our struggles teach us valuable lessons about strength and courage.

It's a Journey: Building resilience doesn't happen overnight. It involves taking care of ourselves, reaching out for support, and finding tools like journaling to help us reflect and heal.

13. Curiosity (Lime Green)

Try New Things: Jumping into new activities, even if they feel a bit out of reach, can really boost both your physical and mental well-being. For example, starting yoga might be tough at first, but the benefits for your back and peace of mind can be undeniable.

Let Curiosity Lead: Allowing your curiosity to guide you can open up a world of new experiences, enriching your life significantly. Whether it's a new hobby or cultural exploration, it makes every day more exciting and fulfilling.

Face Your Fears: By actively engaging in new experiences, you'll start to dismantle your fears and build real confidence. From experimenting with different healing techniques to exploring philosophical ideas, taking these steps can transform your outlook and strengthen your spirit.

14. Connection (Pink)

Strength In Community: Being part of groups like Weight Watchers or a support group for parents of children with autism shows how shared challenges can bring people together, offering support and inspiration.

Choose Your Circle Wisely: The people you hang out with can really shape your life. Spending time with positive folks can boost your mood and help you reach your goals.

Setting Boundaries: It's okay to have limits with friends and family who don't see eye-to-eye with you. Clear boundaries help keep these relationships healthy without stopping your personal progress.

15. Joy (Yellow)

Gratitude Reveals Hidden Joys: The practice of gratitude can lead to the discovery of joy in unexpected places. By focusing on what you're thankful for, you may start to notice the small, often overlooked details in your daily life that bring happiness, leading to a deeper appreciation for the present moment.

Gratitude Can Change Your Outlook: Even if you're skeptical at first, regularly writing down what you're thankful for can transform your outlook. It turns out that noticing and appreciating the simple things can make life feel richer and more enjoyable.

Spreading Gratitude Feels Great: Sharing your gratitude isn't just good for you; it lifts others up, too. Whether it's a smile, a thank you, or a kind note, showing gratitude makes a big difference in your community and circles.

My hope is that you don't tuck this book away on a shelf to gather dust and then eventually donate it, or heaven forbid, throw it out! This is your guidebook, and the chapters, activities, and journal prompts can and should be revisited. I know from experience how I can get all pumped up after reading something only to forget the title a week later. This is too important to allow that to happen. Even if you have already completed an activity, repeating it at a different time usually brings about new answers and revelations. The same goes for rereading different "sprinkles" when you need a refresher.

I wrote this book, first and foremost, because I want to see you live your life to the fullest, whatever that looks like for you. I have absolute faith and confidence in you, but I wanted to make sure you had the tools to get started. This book is just the beginning. I'm constantly creating things to help you on your journey, so stay connected with me by checking out my website: www.DebbieRWeiss.com.

I have to leave you with my favorite quote from Glinda the Good Witch in *The Wizard of Oz*, who said:

"You've always had the power, my dear; you just had to learn it for yourself."

Here's to new beginnings and to you living your most vibrant, extraordinary life. Grab those sprinkles and make it happen—your amazing future is waiting!

Acknowledgments

Writing a book can be a daunting, lonely job. It's you, your thoughts, and a computer in a quiet room trying to relay your message to your audience in a way that will be entertaining but useful. No one is in the room with you, giving you feedback like you would when speaking to a group. You can't tell if they will laugh at the part that was supposed to be funny or shed a tear when sharing a poignant moment. You sit alone, wondering if anyone will ever read this and if my intended message will be delivered. However, even though it's my story, my words, and my message, I'm happy to say I was never truly alone and couldn't have done it without the support of many.

If you had told me back in 2021 that I would become an author, I would have laughed out loud and told you there wasn't a chance in hell. Now I can trace my author roots back several years to when I began to listen to podcasts, eventually landing on the Primal Potential Podcast with Elizabeth Benton as a favorite. I don't personally know Elizabeth, but somehow I feel like I do. She led me to Chris and Lori Harder, who, through their Fast Foundations Mastermind, opened the door to an online world of amazing people I never knew existed. In that mastermind, I met Erin O'Connor, Happy Humans Mindfulness; Sarah Jansel, Jansel and Co; Sarah Hines (@thesarahhines); Andrea Crisp, host of The Couragecast podcast; and Alex Street author of Storyarc, who have all become my friends, confidantes, and cheerleaders even though we have never met in person. It was Sarah Jansel who introduced me to Shana Recker (@iamshanarecker), who became my business coach and so much more in early 2021. Shana put the book idea in my head, but I resisted—that is, until I heard another podcast.

Listening to Powerhouse Women, I heard Lindsey Schwartz interview Lauren Eckhardt from Burning Soul Press. Lauren was launching a group for first-time authors to help them get their stories out there. Lauren, as well as fellow author Alexis Carpenter, were both always there, encouraging and pushing me. Our weekly meetings kept me inspired and on track. Allison Buehner and Katie Talpos were amazing editors. They sprinkled their own brand of magic on my words and cleaned them up a bit.

From there, the book went to my group of beta readers, who volunteered their time to read my book and provide feedback. A huge thank you to them! Behind the scenes, Lenora Henson and Kennedy Marley have been a tremendous support and have kept me on track.

It may seem silly to thank Oprah Winfrey, especially since I don't know her personally (*yet!*). However, she has inspired millions, including me, and we all have the choice of how to use that inspiration to fuel our own lives. I have listened to and watched her inspiring journey, as well as the stories she shared with thousands of people. Her lifelong battle with weight resonates with me deeply, as it's an experience only truly understood by those who have lived it. Throughout my life, she has appeared in moments when I needed her wisdom the most. Over the past decade, I have chosen not only to listen but also to take action.

I feel like the luckiest person on earth because I have the most loving and incredible support from my family and friends. They are there to lift me up when I need lifting, laugh with me, and cry with me. They put me in my place when necessary while still making me feel loved. Mom, Michael, Tracie, Aunt Judy, Mindy, Pam, Mary, and Wheezie—each of you helps me in different ways to keep going, not just in writing but in living. There are no other people I'd rather share my life with. I love you guys! In addition, there are many others whose love and support has meant the world to me. I couldn't have done this without you. Thank you!

Then there's my incredible team at my insurance office: Mary Jo, Helen, Kathy, and Robin. Day in and day out, they are there helping our customers, but they don't do it for the money (although, of course, that's part of it). They truly care about helping people, and without their love and support, I could never have set off to chase my dreams.

Becoming a mom was something I dreamed about from a very young age. It took me a long time to get there, but thanks to IVF, I did, and I was given the two greatest gifts in my life— Sam and Ben. I'm incredibly proud that you are both so kind, loving, and caring. Even though right now you might not be interested in reading any of my books (wink! wink!), someday you will, and I want you to know that you are the inspiration behind all I do.

Thank you to those I mourn and miss every day. You have all impacted my life in countless ways and helped shape the person I am today. I love you, Dad, Joe, and Poppy. And my husband, Gary, who, even though he is still with me in spirit, my heart is forever broken. A happy memory, an argument, and your last days play over and over in my mind like a broken record. What I wouldn't do to have the old Gary back for just one more day.

Last but not least, thank you to my Facebook community, followers, clients, and YOU, the reader. You show me that what I share is meaningful and helpful. I hope this book helps you live a more colorful and fulfilling life, just as I am now.

About the Author

Debbie is a bestselling author, speaker, coach, and course creator with over 60 years of experience overcoming life's challenges. As a family caregiver for over 40 years, a widow, and the mother of two boys in their twenties, Debbie draws from deep personal experience in her mission to help others. She is the author of the memoir *On Second Thought, Maybe I Can...* and a contributor to the Amazon bestseller *Heart Whispers*. In addition to her writing, Debbie operates an insurance agency and runs the online store *A Sprinkle of Hearts*. She also hosts the *Maybe I Can* podcast, where she shares her journey and insights to inspire others.

Debbie is a Certified Canfield Trainer in *The Success Principles*, bringing a wealth of knowledge and proven strategies to her coaching and presentations. She is passionate about helping people overcome their limiting beliefs and fears, lose the victim mentality, and take control of their lives despite their circumstances. Whether through her books, courses, or speaking engagements, Debbie aims to unlock the potential in every individual she connects with.

In her leisure time, she enjoys traveling, going to the beach, reading, and staying active. Debbie's ultimate mission is to inspire others to embrace their unique journeys and create a more colorful and fulfilling life.

Connect with Debbie

www.debbierweiss.com

@debbie.r.weiss.com

@debbierweiss

facebook.com/groups/maybeican

linkedin.com/in/debbieweiss/

tiktok.com/@debbierweiss

Discover your life purpose with a free visualization meditation from Debbie.
Visit debbierweiss.com/visualization

Made in United States
North Haven, CT
13 February 2025